BEST SCHOOL in the WORLD

BEST SCHOOL in the WORLD

HOW STUDENTS, TEACHERS AND PARENTS HAVE CREATED A MODEL THAT CAN TRANSFORM CANADA'S PUBLIC SCHOOLS

Molly Hurd

FORMAC PUBLISHING COMPANY LIMITED
HALIFAX

Copyright © 2017 by Molly Hurd

All rights reserved. No part of this book may be reproduced or transmitted in any form or by any means, electronic or mechanical, including photocopying, or by any information storage or retrieval system, without permission in writing from the publisher.

Formac Publishing Company Limited recognizes the support of the Province of Nova Scotia through the Department of Communities, Culture and Heritage - Creative Industries Fund. We are pleased to work in partnership with the Province of Nova Scotia to develop and promote our cultural resources for all Nova Scotians. We acknowledge the support of the Canada Council for the Arts, which last year invested $153 million to bring the arts to Canadians throughout the country. This project has been made possible in part by the Government of Canada.

Cover design: Tyler Cleroux

All cover and interior photos courtesy of Molly Hurd or Halifax Independent School, except pages: 122 (Globoforce.com), 127 & 128 (Mandai Mohan), 146 (New Brunswick Government), 211 (Heather Beall).

Library and Archives Canada Cataloguing in Publication

 Hurd, Molly, author
    Best school in the world : how students, teachers and parents have created a model that can transform Canada's public schools / Molly Hurd.

Includes bibliographical references and index.
Issued in print and electronic formats.
ISBN 978-1-4595-0468-4 (softcover).--ISBN 978-1-4595-0469-1 (EPUB)

    1. Halifax Independent School. 2. Private schools--Nova Scotia--Halifax. 3. Education--Nova Scotia--Halifax. I. Title.

LC51.2.N68H87 2017   371.0209716'225   C2017-900794-7
                                                                                                                           C2017-900795-5

Formac Publishing Company Limited
5502 Atlantic Street,
Halifax, Nova Scotia, Canada
B3H 1G4
www.formac.ca

Printed and bound in Canada.

CONTENTS

INTRODUCTION — 7

Chapter 1
LEARNING AND LOVING IT THROUGH INTEGRATED INQUIRY TEACHING — 23

Chapter 2
SNEAKING THE LEARNING IN: LITERACY IN AN INTEGRATED ENVIRONMENT — 56

Chapter 3
FIGURING IT OUT: HANDS-ON MATHEMATICS — 93

Chapter 4
NOT JUST FRILLS — ARTS EDUCATION — 120

Chapter 5
SECOND-LANGUAGE LEARNING — 138

Chapter 6
THE WHOLE CHILD: SOCIO-EMOTIONAL LEARNING — 155

Chapter 7
MEASURING UP: AUTHENTIC ASSESSMENT — 190

Chapter 8
WHAT TEACHERS NEED: AUTONOMY, TRUST AND A CULTURE OF COLLABORATION — 214

CONCLUSION — 251

ACKNOWLEDGEMENTS — 263

ENDNOTES — 265

INDEX — 276

To my dad, Allan Hurd, who taught me to question

INTRODUCTION

> *"Since we can't know what knowledge will be most needed in the future, it is senseless to try to teach it in advance. So instead, we should try to turn out people who love learning so much and learn so well that they will be able to learn whatever needs to be learned."*
> — *John Holt*, How Children Fail, *1964*

"Best school in the world!" I often heard these words when teaching at Halifax Independent School. Every day, I witnessed children learning and truly loving it. This is what made my job so rewarding, and why so many educators think teaching is the best career in the world.

When our children go off to school, we don't expect their days to be a constant thrill. But most of us hope that they will be happy while learning what they need in the care of someone who truly appreciates them. Many of us, holding our newborns for the first time, have been filled with wonder at the potential that is locked up in these wrinkled, squalling armfuls. We dream about their bright futures. Later we can see, in those explosions of joy when our curious two-year-olds discover something new, how we all start with a love of learning. Virtually all parents hope that their children's education will help them keep this passion for learning and become healthy, happy, fulfilled adults.

Schools play a huge role in children's lives, and the kind of experience they have in them shapes the kind of adults they become. So how can we make sure that schools help them live up to their potential? How can we be sure that children are in the care of teachers who really know them, appreciate them and are able to challenge them to do and be their best? How can we ensure that schools are not just turning children into someone else's idea of what they should be . . . or worse, actively discouraging them from finding their own talents?

Some parents can choose the kind of education their children get — they can afford to pay for private schools, to move to a place where the schools are in tune with their philosophy or they can homeschool their children. But most of us don't have that luxury: the local public school is the only option. And although there are lots of excellent teachers and programs within those schools, too often it seems that public schools are not serving children well. Why?

I have spent most of my life in education in some form. After attending public schools in Ottawa, I went to university in Kingston, obtained a teaching degree in Nova Scotia and then taught in aboriginal communities and Nigeria for six years. Upon returning to Canada, I worked in promoting global education in schools and did substitute teaching in Ottawa and Nova Scotia. But it was not until I began working at the tiny Dalhousie University School in 1992 that my education about education truly started.

Dalhousie University School, later called the Dalhousie Co-operative School and still later Halifax Independent School, is a "progressive" school that began in the 1970s, in the heyday of free schools, whole language and child-centred education. Located in the education building at Dalhousie, it was a wonderful place to teach and learn, and there were days I would pinch myself that I had been so lucky to stumble upon it. Several key ingredients made it such a great place for teachers and children: teachers had the freedom to plan the curriculum; the school was run by parents and teachers, but the teachers were respected as the "experts" on education; the school prioritized the whole child, and their intellectual, emotional, physical and social development; and finally, an atmosphere of trust and good will assumed that everyone, from parents and teachers down to the tiniest child, was doing their best.

The philosophy of theme studies was developed at Halifax Independent during the 1980s and 1990s, and it is described in some detail in an earlier book about the school, *Learning and Loving It: Theme Studies in the Classroom*.[1] Theme studies is just one of a number of progressive philosophies, but it is the one that I know best. It integrates core subjects into the study of "themes" (topics of interest to children), and enables them to develop the tools for making sense of the world around them in a holistic, cohesive way. This creates the "aha!" moments that both enhance their enjoyment of learning and make the experiences more memorable. They then become motivated to learn the skills necessary to pursue their interests and share them with others. In the early years, reading and writing become the keys to unlock the world of knowledge that the teacher introduces; once children master these basic skills, others take their place — research skills, computer literacy, debating, making presentations and more.

Over the twenty years I taught at this small, independent school, I observed the public system move steadily in the opposite direction. Curricula became more prescribed and centralized. Schools and parents had less control over what happened at the local level — boards made decisions to reorganize that went against the wishes of whole communities. Teachers in the system were marginalized in decision making and, as a result, more often felt burnt out and unappreciated. As more emphasis was placed on test results and quantifiable outcomes, a focus on the individual child was often lost. And, finally, a dismal drumbeat of media stories about deadbeat teachers, greedy unions and the need to make the system "accountable" fostered a lack of trust in the very people to whom we send our children every school day.

At Halifax Independent School, we saw the fallout from this process in the transfers from other schools: the children, diagnosed with special needs in the public system, who just needed to be engaged in something that interested them; the sensitive, quiet child whose emotional needs were on no one's radar; the self-motivated student who was constantly having to wait for the rest of the class to catch up. And then there were the parents, bruised from fighting and losing to a school board over the closure of a small school or a special needs diagnosis.

It all convinced me that Halifax Independent School was a little haven of sanity and humanness in an educational environment that was increasingly bureaucratized and insensitive. It was a place where the teachers were free to exercise their creativity and put their knowledge of child development to use in designing curricula aimed not only at children's intellectual needs, but their social, emotional and physical needs as well — in short, to practise the kind of education they were trained for.

But how is this relevant to the rest of the world? Halifax Independent School is a private school where parents can afford the fees. When it was a cooperative, we struggled to keep the fees low and involved everyone . . . that was easier. But by the time we had expanded enough that we were able to build a new building, we needed to keep the fees high enough to cover our expenses. Sometimes we had to turn children away who couldn't afford the tuition, and that was disheartening.

Yet, the longer I stayed at Halifax Independent School, the more I became convinced that all children could benefit from this type of education, and in fact, that all children deserve it. I watched those refugees from the public system fit right in to Halifax Independent School and thrive. I felt that there was no reason that public schools couldn't provide this kind of holistic, child-centred education. The annual tuition Halifax Independent School charged, even after moving into its own building, remained approximately on par with the amount the Nova Scotia government spent on education per child each year. So it's not hugely expensive to do this type of progressive education. Why then do so many public school systems seem to be moving in the opposite direction — to be getting less progressive, more centrally controlled and less oriented to what the children need? Why does school seem to fail so many students?

The contradictory views about education we see or read in the media are bewildering. Are small classes important for optimal learning, or does class size have no effect? Should teachers be trusted to do their jobs, or do schools need top-down administration to crack down and make them more accountable? Should we be extending the school year or day to give more hours for learning time or should we let children play more? What do we want our kids to learn, anyway?

This book will answer these questions and look at how Halifax Independent has managed to develop and refine its progressive philosophy over the years. I am a great believer in public education and equality of opportunity, and I believe it is possible that what works at Halifax Independent can work in any school. Although I have not taught extensively in public schools in Canada, I have taught in them in Britain and Tanzania, and have been a parent of two children educated in public schools in Nova Scotia. I will draw on all these educational experiences plus the research I have done over the years to reflect on what has made Halifax Independent so successful, and what aspects are transferable to public education in Canada.

TRADITIONAL VERSUS PROGRESSIVE EDUCATION

Two main streams of thought have influenced education in the twentieth century. The traditional or behaviourist approach sees children as "tabula rasa" (clean slates), or empty vessels to be filled with knowledge and skills whether they are willing or not. The teacher's job is to provide the knowledge and teach the skills. The results can be measured on standardized tests, and the job of educational administrators is to monitor test results to make sure teachers are doing their jobs.

The progressive or constructivist approach is fundamentally different. It sees humans as a species that is hard-wired for curiosity and children as individuals who actively try to make sense of new information — i.e., children want to learn. Schools work best when they build on, and foster, the innate curiosity of children. The role of teachers is to create the opportunities that enable the children to learn.

Traditional Classrooms	Constructivist Classrooms
1. Curriculum is presented part to whole with emphasis on **basic** skills.	1. Curriculum is presented whole to part, with emphasis on big **concepts.**
2. Strict adherence to **fixed** curriculum is highly valued.	2. Pursuit of student **questions** is highly valued.
3. Curricular activities rely heavily on **textbooks** and workbooks.	3. Materials include primary sources and **manipulatives.**
4. Students are viewed as **"blank slates"** onto which information is etched by the teacher.	4. Students are viewed as **thinkers** with emerging theories about the world.
5. Teachers generally behave in a **didactic** manner, disseminating information to the students.	5. Teachers generally behave in an **interactive** manner, mediating the environment for students.
6. Teachers seek the **correct answer** to validate student learning.	6. Teachers seek the **students' points of view** in order to understand students' present conceptions for use in subsequent lessons.
7. Assessment of student learning is viewed as **separate** from teaching and occurs almost entirely through **testing.**	7. Assessment of student learning is **interwoven** with teaching and occurs through teacher observations of students at work and through students' **exhibitions and portfolios.**
8. Students work primarily **alone**.	8. Students work primarily in **groups**.

From Dr. Jennifer Irwin[2]

Like many other disciplines, educational theory has swung pendulum-like between the two schools of thought. The early 1970s saw some radical changes in the way we look at education. Writers such as John Dewey, AS Neill, John Holt and Paulo Freire turned the traditional view upside down, and progressive, child-centred schools popped up all over the world. Educational research began to look more closely into how children learn, and then at the best ways to teach them. New methodologies were tried. Some worked well and have become standard practice in many schools, some still exist in individual schools and many others faded away entirely.

Dalhousie University School (now Halifax Independent School) was originally one of a number of "laboratory" schools that became popular around that time, and were initially envisioned as teacher training schools and centres for research. Some of them still exist — for example, Eric Jackman School in Toronto is associated with the Ontario Institute for Studies in Education (OISE). These two schools, Eric Jackman and Halifax Independent School, share many progressive aspects and are thriving. Unfortunately, while these schools were developing and adapting their progressive methodologies, the tide was turning the other way in public education.

BACK TO BASICS, AGAIN

In the mid-1970s, Britain was a leader in progressive education. While I was doing my teaching degree, we looked to British schools as a model — open classrooms, child-centred learning and the integrated day were just some of the things we read about. Unfortunately, the British system had little time to develop and extend this experiment before a backlash in the 1980s. The term "child-centred education" was suddenly turned into code for wishy-washy, anything-goes time wasting. By the end of the 1980s, British education was transformed into a very traditional, centrally controlled system. The pendulum had swung back with a vengeance.

By the time I was teaching in Britain in 2001 to 2002, the rout of progressive education was complete. The schools I visited and taught at were grim places. From the head teacher to the youngest student, everyone was on edge — totally focused on the Scholastic Achievement Tests (SATs) and the centrally defined curriculum. While I was there, the "National Literacy Hour" introduced a set of literacy lessons that teachers were expected to stand in front of their classes and deliver every day. These incredibly detailed lessons, created by a national board, included precise words to use and set times for each activity. They were exactly the same for all classes, all over the country — and they certainly did not work for my class. I wondered exactly which children would benefit from this one-size-fits-all model of education.

Education became a tool of the marketplace, producing what it thought "the market" needed. But creativity and critical thinking were not part of their vision, nor was ensuring that children loved learning and could develop the future skills that an ever-changing world would need. In these "reforms," the process of learning was reduced to preparing children to answer test questions correctly. Huge amounts of education spending were devoted to creating, administering and interpreting these standardized tests. But the needs of individual children were left behind.

The British reforms are an example of what has been called the Global Education Reform Movement (GERM)[3] of the 2000s, which also spawned "No Child Left Behind" and the "Race for the Top" in the US. This movement, which ironically started with the idealistic goal to give every child the same opportunity, actually ended up entrenching inequality in the system. At the same time, it has done nothing to improve standings on international educational comparisons.

In Canada we have often imported ideas from the UK and the US. Fortunately, Canada has not yet travelled as far down the path of standardized education as these countries have. Although standardized testing has increased dramatically since the 1970s, most school boards in Canada have not reached the point of using standardized test results as sticks with which to beat school administrators or carrots to reward so-called excellent teachers or schools. This is happening in both the UK and the US, where poorly performing schools are at risk of closing, and boards are considering merit pay for teachers.

But has that been working for them? Are American and British schools actually getting better at teaching children what they need to know? How do they fare internationally? How do they stack up against Canada and other countries?

Canada consistently outstrips both countries on most international educational measures by large margins. One of the most important international comparisons, the Programme for International Student Assessment (PISA)[4] done by the Organisation for Economic Co-operation and Development (OECD), tests a representative sample of fifteen-year-olds from sixty-five countries every three years. They measure "what students know and can do" in reading, mathematics and science, but also give extensive questionnaires to gather data on many other aspects of students' lives. Socio-economic status, attendance records at school, education level of teachers and amount spent by the government on education are just a few examples of the types of data collected.

Over the years, the PISA studies have generated a huge amount of information about educational policy and have become more influential. Some of their clearest findings show that many of the characteristics of the GERM systems are actually correlated with poorer academic performance. Canada, however, scores very highly overall, usually ranking in the top ten countries in the fifteen years the tests have been administered. Canada also consistently tops all the high-performing countries in equity: doing well in school here is not as dependent on what strata of society one comes from as it is in many more unequal countries.[5]

But the big finding for me was the discovery of Finland's education miracle. In the first PISA study in 2000, Finland came out on top out of the forty-three OECD countries. It had earlier radically reformed its education system, borrowing many progressive aspects from Canadian and British schools of the previous era. The aim of these reforms was not to produce better results on international academic tests, but to make sure that every child in the country was given an equal opportunity to succeed in the school system — in other words, to achieve equity in education. The excellence was a side effect.

But what I found most amazing about Finland's education system was that it possessed many characteristics that Halifax Independent School had independently evolved — even down to the structure. (Finland's "peruskoulu" schools generally cover the first nine years of education in one building, as does Halifax Independent School.) The PISA data has enabled the OECD to show rigorously what I had long suspected from practical experience: that some characteristics of schools — such as highly trained, respected teachers; a lack of stratification (streaming); making sure that all children are taught according to their needs; collaboration among teachers and local school control over curricula and assessments — actually produce better academic results in international comparisons. So why do GERM countries continue down the same path, despite most research about child development as well as the evidence provided by international comparative studies such as PISA? We are not immune to GERM here in Canada — in recent years, provincial governments have exerted more control over curricula and demanded more "accountability" from teachers and school boards. Why has education become more "traditional" than it was forty years ago? This book will look at the some of the factors at play in Canadian education, and using Halifax

Independent School as an example, will correct some of the prevalent myths about progressive education that have contributed to this.

TWENTY-FIRST-CENTURY SKILLS

I have taught in Northern Quebec, rural Nova Scotia, Nigeria, Tanzania, Britain and, for the past twenty years, at the Halifax Independent School. Every classroom that I have gone into has consisted of a collection of unique individuals, with different learning styles, personalities, developmental rates and attitudes. Standardized education is doomed to fail most children, and even those who do "well" in this system are getting a less rich education than they should. All young people deserve an education that prepares and challenges them intellectually, emotionally and spiritually to become contributing members of a democratic society. A rich education provides many benefits to the students, including preparing them for, eventually, getting a good job.

The irony is that traditional education does not even prepare children well for the market realities of the twenty-first century. The marketplace that our children will face will be very different from that envisioned by the architects of GERM. Educators, business leaders and technology experts alike know that the world of the future will need motivated, creative workers who are able to cooperate and solve complex problems.

More and more contemporary educational thinkers, such as Sir Ken Robinson, are saying traditional schools are actually killing creativity.[6] Numerous attempts to define twenty-first-century skills have been made, but one offshoot of the National Education Association in the

US, the Partnership for 21st Century Skills, has come up with a simplified list of essential skills — the "Four Cs": *communication*, *critical thinking*, *creativity* and *collaboration*. These skills are what most progressive schools, Halifax Independent School included, aim to teach students, and have been doing for the past forty years. In addition to these, important though they are, I'd like to add three more Cs, attitudes that are equally important: *curiosity* (loving learning), *caring* (about the world and each other) and discovering one's *capacities*.

Using Halifax Independent School as an example, this book aims to describe how learning and loving it is possible for every child. It will give parents and other interested citizens some ideas about how we can help education in Canada become more progressive so that every child in the country can go to their own "best school."

OVERVIEW OF THE BOOK

Critics of progressive education claim that children in progressive schools learn the basic skills haphazardly at best and sometimes not at all. The first three chapters of the book illustrate how wrong that is. Careful curriculum design can build on children's innate desire to learn, so that children learn the basic skills of literacy and numeracy as they get on with learning about what they are interested in. As well, the traditional school has a strict timetable of when students should learn specific skills, and these are tested repeatedly. This means that many children lose out if they are not ready when the curriculum says they should be or they are bored when they develop skills too quickly. A progressive school, on the other hand, recognizes the differing developmental levels, learning styles and interests of each child and adjusts its benchmarks to keep students feeling stimulated but not overwhelmed.

Chapter 1 shows how a method like theme studies or inquiry learning integrates the learning of basic skills with science, literature, social studies and other interesting topics so that children love doing it. Chapter 2 looks at how literacy can be presented so that when they are ready, children learn to love reading and writing, and do lots of it. Chapter 3 describes how mathematics can be taught in a hands-on, problem-solving way so that children uncover the basic principles for themselves — which actually leads to deeper understanding, and is enjoyable at the same time. Children don't have to hate math! All three chapters use real examples to show that the basics don't suffer while children are learning the seven Cs of twenty-first-century skills and attitudes.

One of the casualties of the increased focus on standardized testing in GERM countries is the teaching of the arts. Although new research is showing the huge benefits of arts education, Canadian schools are also cutting back. Chapter 4 looks at how Halifax Independent integrates the arts into all aspects of the curriculum, but at the same time provides a rich program with specialist teachers.

In Canada, being comfortable in a second or third language has huge impacts on one's career prospects, as well as recognized intellectual benefits. Chapter 5 investigates some of the ways in which French is taught in Canada. It describes how the theme or project-based approach to core French teaching at Halifax Independent aims to give children solid communication skills to pave the way to future bilingualism. It also points out ways that the huge resources spent on early immersion programs could be better used to create a more equitable system that could allow more children to achieve functional bilingualism.

As schools become more competitive and teachers are busier and more stressed, the emotional and social needs of children can take a back seat to their academic achievements. Chapter 6 explores the ways parents and teachers can create a school climate in which the uniqueness of each child's multi-faceted personality is respected, shared values are articulated and children learn the skills of cooperation, conflict resolution and how to live in a democracy.

If the purpose of assessment is to help children learn, assessing a child's progress does not have to be about tests, report cards or competition. In fact, it is much more effective when it is authentic and understandable by children. Chapter 7 describes what authentic assessment is, and how it can help children (and their parents) to identify their strengths and weaknesses.

As we have learned from the PISA studies (and from Halifax Independent School), one of the most important contributors to academic success is teacher autonomy, collaboration and engagement. Chapter 8 shows how a partnership and respect between teachers, parents and the community can build excellence in progressive education. A case study of a holistic educational experience, "Mini-Society," developed over the years at Halifax Independent School, is presented as an example of what can happen when teachers and parents are engaged, motivated and free to be creative and collaborative.

Educational change can be sudden and dramatic, as it was in the 1970s, but more often it has been incremental and subtle. Shrinking budgets, more government control and the marginalization of teachers are some of the trends in Canada that could combine to work against the type of progressive education that allows many children to achieve their potential and acquire a lifelong love of learning. What I have learned from my time at Halifax Independent School has convinced me that we need more progressive education in Canada, not less.

Chapter 1
LEARNING AND LOVING IT THROUGH INTEGRATED INQUIRY TEACHING

> *"Never underestimate the vital importance of finding early in life the work that for you is play. This turns possible underachievers into happy warriors."*
> — Sir Ken Robinson, The Element: How Finding Your Passion Changes Everything

On a dreary, early December morning, the parents gathering in the front lobby of Halifax Independent School can feel a buzz of excitement that seems to come from the very walls of the school.

Above, the sounds of children singing waft from the music room, and across the hall tables and benches in the lunchroom are being moved to create an open space. The "Work-a-ma-jig," a kinetic sculpture designed and made by all the students in the school a few years before, is lit up and ready for action. Down the hall, glass classroom doors are covered with cloth and signs saying, "No Parnts Aloud." This is no ordinary day at Halifax Independent — it is Fair Day!

One of the many unique aspects of Halifax Independent School is the way the multi-age classes are named. Originally, there were just three classes: the Youngs (four- and five-year-olds), the Middles (six- and seven-year-olds) and the Olds (eight- and nine-year-olds). As the school grew, the Littles were added (four-year-olds), and the Elders (ten-and eleven-year-olds). Finally, around 2003, the middle school was started, with its more prosaic names: Middle School 1, 2 and 3, corresponding to Grades 7, 8 and 9.

Throughout the day, each class will unveil their transformed classrooms and treat their parents and other interested people to a presentation about the "theme" they have been studying for the past three months. Fair is the culmination of the children's research, the showcasing of their knowledge and talents and a chance for them to hone their presentation skills. Let's take a walk around and visit some of these presentations.

We start in the six- and seven-year-olds' class (the Middles) in which one whole corner has been built up into a "rocky" ledge, around which various little tide pool animals are perched (the giggles let us know that these are in fact children, hidden under foam headpieces). Two children with a papier-mâché microphone enter and begin to interview the creatures. One by one they stand up and tell the enraptured audience about their unique habits and characteristics. A song written by the children finishes up the formal presentation, whereupon the parents are invited to view the exhibits of research booklets, models and artwork.

Upstairs, the eight- and nine-year-olds (the Olds) are taking their parents on a trip to the depths of the Gully, a Marine Protected Area off the coast of Sable Island that is rich in marine life. As parents enter the classroom, they must climb through the "hatch" and take their seats in the Remotely Operated Vehicle, which has been created in the centre of the room. Then, as the lights dim, they are invited to imagine they are descending hundreds of metres underwater. A spotlight illuminates the black sheets covering the classroom wall, which are decorated with paintings of beautiful deep-sea coral. A succession of underwater creatures then appears, telling the audience about their habitat, life cycle, place on the food chain, migration and finally about the environmental threats they face.

The ten- and eleven-year-olds (the Elders), dressed as various animals or adult "types," are attending a town hall meeting to decide whether a new highway should be built that would cut directly across Shannon Salt Marsh, the last remaining salt marsh in the area. A large model of the wetland, labelled with the various habitats, is in the centre of the room. Everyone gets their say: environmentalists, the department of highways, the tourism association, the business association, farmers and even the "Calico Clams." After listening to all the presentations, the parents (who are playing the roles of the councillors) have to vote on four different options: to go ahead with the department of highways' proposal, to conduct further studies to determine the effects of highways on the area, to develop the marsh for tourism or to declare the marsh a protected zone.

We wander around, listen to the parents' comments and see the proud glow on the children's faces. We view the artistically presented displays and listen in on little "experts" answering complex questions on their areas of authority. We wonder, "How did all this happen?"

To answer that question, let's look at the lead up to the Fair, the first three months of the school year. The school-wide theme this year is "Oceans" and each classroom teacher in the elementary department guided their classes through the in-depth study of various ocean-related sub-themes.

Early in the term, the six- and seven-year-olds made several visits to beaches in the area and investigated the different ecosystems at the shoreline. They paid particular attention to the tide pools and later visited a touch tank at Dalhousie University, where they could handle various creatures of the shoreline: crabs, clams, mussels, sea cucumbers and starfish. After exploring the ecosystem in general through books, guest speakers and films, the children selected one creature each to study, then gathered information on it for a research book. Along the way, they wrote poetry, painted pictures, created clay models, wrote stories in which their creature was the main character and read other fictional stories and myths about tide pool animals. The products of their work are all displayed, and parents can view the progression of their child's writing skills in the research books. Finally, in preparation for Fair Day, they made headpieces to represent their creature and wrote a song about tide pools.

The eight- and nine-year-olds had visited the Bedford Institute of Oceanography, where they saw a special exhibit about the Gully and its deep-sea corals. There were models of the ocean floor, dioramas of underwater scenes and lots of experts to answer questions. They learned about how oceanographic research was conducted, and heard stories about the research vessel *Hudson*. Later, in class, they interviewed some PhD students who had spent the summer studying bottlenose whales, one of the types of whales that visit the Gully. They each chose a sea creature living in the Gully and, using non-fiction books and an interactive CD for research, wrote and illustrated books about their creature. In groups, they researched the different types of deep-sea corals, and then featured these in detailed, painted wall

Visit to the Dalhousie oceanography department.

murals. They watched movies about undersea exploration, and, as a class, created the control panel of a remotely operated underwater vehicle that decorated the frame in which their parents were seated during Fair Day. They read articles about the environmental threats facing the Gully, and heard about the school's earlier involvement in having the Gully made a Marine Protected Area. Finally, they wrote a play for the annual school Plays based on their research in the Gully.

The ten- and eleven-year-olds had been studying coastal ecosystems, and in particular the salt marsh ecosystem. Along the way, they posed the question, "Why are salt marshes so important?" To find out, they used a local environmental organization's activity pack[7] as a resource to develop the town hall scenario described above. They did extensive research on the area's various life forms, but then carried it further as they looked at the human impact and needs for the area. They chose roles and researched them, writing speeches that a person/animal in that position might give at the town hall meeting. Not only did these students learn about the various issues involved in each of the roles, they learned about persuasive writing and gained insight into the public consultation process.

Any visitor to the school would see how engaged all the children are — but this does not happen only at Fair time. They have produced an impressive amount of "work," which shows a progression in their skill level — and not just in the basics, but for more advanced skills. Perhaps their written sentences are longer than at the last Fair, their presentations more confident, their drawings more detailed, their grasp of how government works deeper. Parents can certainly notice the growth of their children's knowledge and interest in the subject matter.

Theme studies is just one example of a progressive methodology — there are probably as many varieties as there are progressive schools. What makes it, and other progressive methodologies, effective?

HOW AND WHY DOES PROGRESSIVE EDUCATION WORK?

All progressive methodologies capitalize on students' innate curiosity and drive to learn. The curriculum is rooted in authentic situations that give students a sense of contributing to something real, and they are given control over their own learning through real choices. Students work in cooperative groups, allowing lots of social interaction. They are encouraged to formulate questions and find many sources of information to answer them. The teacher acts as a facilitator, providing experiences, guiding the process and supporting the students in their learning; one of his or her key roles is to ensure that students are motivated and developing the core skills.

Contrast this with what happens in many traditional schools. Traditional education serves a main course of literacy and math skills to students, with a side order of knowledge chunks deemed necessary for a minimally balanced pedagogic diet. The core knowledge chunks — usually science, social studies and health — come with a set of guidelines and curriculum outlines, often based on a particular text or program. Each subject has a long list of specific "learning outcomes" to be assessed and checked off, and each is usually taught completely separately from the other core subjects. In this view of education, the definition of what constitutes a balanced diet may change, but the idea that students are empty vessels, waiting to be filled, never wavers. The teachers' job is to make sure that these vessels are filled efficiently, and tests measure how well they have done their job. This can be pretty unappetizing for the students, even if the diet is relatively balanced.

How often have we known children who start out school at age five, full of excitement, but then after a few years are unenthusiastic or actively dislike school? It is so common that we often think of it as a natural part of growing up, a sort of developmental stage, the "hating-school stage." Yet it doesn't have to be like this.

In a traditional science classroom, for example, children are generally given information from a text or other source. Then they are given an assignment based on the information, usually questions whose answers will be found in the text/information source. They write up the answers, and are later tested on those answers. It is simple — information in, information out.

Progressive classrooms tend to turn this sequence on its head. A progressive teacher will start out with the idea that the children want to learn about a particular topic (they usually have some element of choice in what they learn), and will give them experiences that spark questions and interest. She doesn't profess to know everything about the topic, nor does she know exactly where the investigation will lead. Together with her class, she will design a course of learning that may include generating questions, designing experiments, researching various sources and producing a final product that will have a real purpose. The test will be in how the final product works.

Progressive education, or constructivism, views the child not as an empty vessel, but as an innately curious, whole being who actively tries to make sense of new information. By engaging the whole child — their curiosity, their emotions and their senses — it aims to create a love of learning that will last a lifetime. At Halifax Independent School, by integrating the "main course" of literacy and the "side order" parts of the curriculum, theme studies provides a holistic context that more closely matches the way children actually learn, making it enjoyable and showing that a wholesome diet can actually taste good. Instead of teaching individual subjects separately, literacy, science, social studies, health and the arts are integrated into the study of "themes" or topics.

The five yearly themes at Halifax Independent School — Oceans, the World of Work, Living Things, Discovery and Nova Scotia — were selected because of their breadth, their intrinsic interest to children and their adaptability to cover topics in the social studies and science realms of knowledge. Because the whole school works with the same theme, teachers can collaborate, share resources and create a climate in which everyone can learn from everyone else. And the fact that the whole school is focused on the same subject creates a sense of excitement about learning and the topics (and can generate peer pressure to excel) that even the parents can get swept up in!

> **Case study: Ancient civilizations — Getting started (ages ten and eleven)**
> During the Discovery theme, my Elders class spent a month studying mysteries, with a particular focus on forensic science. A visit to a Saint Mary's University forensic laboratory introduced them to the wonders of doing anthropological and forensic research on bones — they were fascinated by how much could be learned from old human bones. At the same time, a story we read in a book of unsolved mysteries about the disappearance of the Anasazi people in New Mexico led them to a fascination with ancient cultures, an interest I decided to pick up on for our next topic of study.
>
> After lots of discussion, and time for the children to peruse the many library books and other resources I'd provided, we narrowed our possible civilizations to study to six or seven that fit the criteria I had set down: ancient civilizations which were geographically spread around the world, existed more than five hundred years ago and had contributed something major to the world as a whole.
>
> The class then watched a short video about ancient China and the terracotta warriors to give them some ideas about possible areas to investigate. Afterward, we generated questions to be answered about ancient cultures in general, and brainstormed ideas for a final project. They decided that they would like to make models of a typical terracotta house and family of the time, and present their research in the form of giant scrolls to be hung around the classroom.
>
> Once we had chosen the civilizations to be studied, I mapped out a sequence of activities, making sure that all the core subject

An Aztec pyramid and village.

areas were covered. I chose creative writing topics, found a novel to read aloud (*Pirates of Pompeii* by Caroline Lawrence) and selected some readings. Construction methods for the models that would involve new skills were investigated. To make the houses, I consulted with the art teacher, and we decided that we would try a method involving plaster bandages (used to make plaster casts) to give a textured effect for the walls. For the model people and small artefacts, I introduced the technique of beeswax modelling (the colourful wax needs to be warmed in the hands, and then carefully molded). I arranged for a field trip to the Department of Classics at Dalhousie University where we had a presentation on ancient Roman culture with a slideshow about Pompeii.

With this clear overview, I was ready to let the children choose their civilization to study, organize the groups and get down to work. We were ready to research!

LEARNING AND LOVING IT THROUGH INTEGRATED INQUIRY TEACHING 33

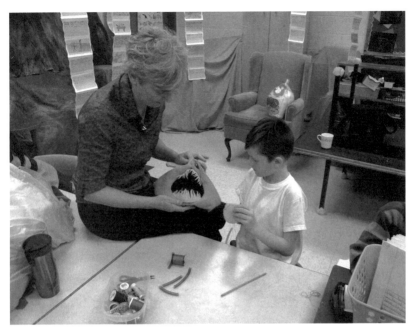

Making stuffed sea creatures with the Middles.

The theme studies approach requires a great deal of planning and collaboration on the part of the teachers, but as *Learning and Loving It* says, it "allows teachers to learn along with the children so that they never become bored with their work."[8] As we will see in Chapter 8, collaborative, happy, respected teachers are crucial to a "good education."

Theme studies shares some of its most important characteristics with most progressive methodologies: motivation, hands-on learning, integration, authentic (real-life) situations and asking good questions.

MOTIVATION: WORK OR PLAY?

> *"Do not keep children to their studies by compulsion but by play."*
>
> — *Plato*

There is a lot written about the importance of motivation in educational literature. How do we motivate children to work hard? Rewards, competitive quizzes and flashy videos have all been used to motivate children in traditional schools. Underlying all this is the assumption that schoolwork is unappetizing and children need motivators to get them to partake. But as Maria Montessori tells us, "play is the work of the child,"[9] and most of us don't have trouble believing so for very young children. Many people think, however, that as soon as they start school, children should get ready for the serious work of education, and that "play" is a diversion or a reward. But the desire to play doesn't stop at age six, and progressive education uses our innate playfulness as a springboard for learning, not as a reward.

Many of us know people who describe loving their work so much it feels like play, and indeed, that is one of the hallmarks of a successful adult. Observe a twelve-year-old shooting baskets in the driveway for hours — is she working or playing? If she loves playing basketball and wants to score for her team in the next game, she may feel like she is playing. If, however, she is on a competitive team and her coach has ordered her to shoot baskets for three hours before the next practice, it is quite possible she will consider it work. Either way, work or play, she is improving her skills.

Progressive schools use play — both unstructured and structured — to keep motivation for learning high. Most educators recognize that children need unstructured playtime (although the move to eliminate recess in some places in the US belies this), but less recognized is the way that structured play can be used in the classroom. Dramatic play is familiar to us in kindergarten, where children may play in a set up "doctor's office" or on a "ship," but is less common in upper-grade classes; however, it is key to keeping children motivated in a progressive classroom. Inventing or partaking in games is another form of structured play.

At Halifax Independent School, a climate of excitement is created around the yearly theme. Because the whole school is studying the same theme, students all get the message that this topic is important, and that everyone — parents, teachers and students — can contribute to the pursuit of this knowledge. In the classroom, the teacher's infectious enthusiasm, inquiring mind and high expectations all help to build this excitement, and they use their knowledge of play to motivate the children. At home, parents often get in on the act by finding resources or family connections that support the theme study. In such an atmosphere, children want to do their best to contribute to the class work; as part of a group, they don't want to let their friends down, and as individuals, they want to shine at Fair for their parents.

In order to keep this excitement for learning alive in any progressive classroom, several things have to happen. First is **differentiated instruction**: nothing squelches enthusiasm faster than when something is just too hard. If a child can't read most of the research material, they will quickly get discouraged. If an activity is too complex or a student doesn't understand the result, frustration can occur. Conversely, if an activity is too simple or does not provide the level of information students want, they can become bored or disengaged. Teachers need to challenge each child, so it is a vital part of their job to provide reading material and activities at appropriate levels for all children, and support for those who need it.

Second, **choice** is extremely important in keeping children engaged and feeling a sense of ownership over their learning. Teachers set the overall direction for a class, but they also provide opportunities for the children to make structured choices over the direction they would like to follow. Some choices are made by the class democratically, after lots of discussion — for instance, whether to focus on either insects or birds in a unit on migration, or to present a final project as a booklet or a poster. Then, there should be an opportunity for individual children to choose a topic for independent research — for example, which tide pool animal they would like to study.

When children feel that their choices have been respected and that they have a say over the course of their learning, they have a **sense of ownership**. At Halifax Independent School, you often hear children talking about "my mineral" or "my sea creature," and this feeling is heightened when they are able to create representations that they can play with creatively. Dioramas, clay figures, stuffed animals, puppets, models and papier-mâché figures all encourage free play and a child's exploration of how "their creature" interacts with its environment. When I was helping the six- and seven-year-olds make stuffed animals of their sea creatures one year, it was quite interesting to see the children spontaneously acting out the food chain — they were very conscious of who eats whom! This identification with, and sometimes emotional attachment to, their object of study adds depth to their learning.

Fourth, **a sense of purpose** is built into all progressive education. At Halifax Independent School, children are very aware that the Fair is the culmination of their study, and an opportunity for them to show their parents what they have learned — to be "experts" on a subject. Other progressive approaches, which also work well, are to design and build something new (design-based learning), to push back the frontiers of knowledge (an inquiry approach), to identify a problem and help effect a change (problem-based learning) or to produce something with an educational purpose (project-based learning). Each of these keeps children motivated and excited about their work.

Finally, it is the teacher who creates and maintains these conditions, and the very nature of the progressive classroom itself. Additionally, the teacher, with support from the parents, cultivates a climate of **high expectations** — the assumption that every child will do their best — and this contributes to the overall thrill of discovery. "High expectations" do not mean that the same results are expected from each child — again, smaller classes mean that the teacher knows the children well, and knows when a child is working to his or her full capacity, which will vary according to individual children. It is important that parents have a realistic sense of what their children can do so that they can support them at home. The child's **sense of pride** when she has done her best is confirmed at the Fair, when parents can share in her success.

At Halifax Independent School, the prospect of the Fair adds some excitement and hence motivation. But the children also learn about working to deadlines, and coping with the heightened sense of pressure that entails. They learn about cooperating with others to achieve a common goal — creating an atmosphere for their ancient cultures exhibit or practising their song until it is word perfect. These are useful life skills. By presenting the subject matter in varied ways — both hands-on and through different types of media — and by offering them a choice in their research topic, their motivation and interest remain high.

In any progressive school, parents have a huge role to play in creating excitement around the topics, in showing interest in what their children are learning, creating high expectations and encouraging their sense of ownership. It was exciting for my class when a child came in on a Monday morning, full of treasures he had collected on the beach over the weekend, and these would be added to the trove of artefacts for the shoreline study we were doing.

Many parents have also supported their children's learning in other concrete ways — a birthday present was often a stuffed animal or a model related to what a child was studying. I remember one father building a model of an Acadian cottage from scratch with his child; she brought it to school, full of pride, and it became the backdrop for an animated video the class made. Many times, children brought in books that they had bought related to the school theme, sometimes with their own money, and these became sources for research. And of course, being the attentive audience at Fair, willing to be surprised and impressed, is essential!

HANDS-ON LEARNING

Hands-on learning goes back to Confucius, who famously said, "I do and I understand." Theme studies provides many opportunities for children to learn by doing as they build, experiment, paint, act out or observe. Parents and the students themselves report on the impact this type of learning has had, and they attest to the fact that the deeper understanding helps them retain and use the information longer.

Working in the school garden.

Beginning a mammal study

Often a hands-on activity will kick off a new study or theme. In the eight- and nine-year-olds' class, each table has a different stuffed animal (borrowed from the local museum) displayed in the centre. The children are seated around, carefully observing, sketching and touching the animal. Lots of chatting is going on:

"I think it eats meat . . . look at those sharp teeth."

"It has thick fur, so it can live in cold places."

"Feel how bristly this fur is!"

"The claws are pretty sharp, so I think they are good fighters."

"It looks like a bandit . . . do you think that is for camouflage?"

The teacher circulates and encourages the children to jot down their observations and questions on their sketches.

Numerous research studies have compared the effects of hands-on learning to traditional teacher-led, lecture and text-based learning. Many of them point out the enhanced problem-solving skills and conceptual understanding resulting from hands-on learning situations.[10] However, equally interesting are the studies showing that children taught using hands-on methodologies actually out-perform those from traditional classrooms on the standardized tests used to measure academic achievement. A recent study at Purdue University[11] compared five Grade 8 science classes who, while doing a unit on water resources, built a water purification system as part of the unit, to a control group studying the same topic through the traditional lecture/text/test method. "In every area we tested, the students who were involved in a hands-on project learned more and demonstrated a deeper understanding of the issues than the traditional group," said the lead investigator.[12] The group doing the hands-on activity also showed significant improvement in two areas: higher levels of thinking on open-ended questions, and greater content knowledge.

Not only did schools using hands-on teaching in outdoor, environmental education situations show better academic performance than control schools, there were also fewer discipline problems, increased engagement and greater pride and ownership in their accomplishments.[13]

But no teacher or parent needs research studies to tell them that allowing children to construct, touch, experiment or create with tangible objects will bump up their level of excitement, engagement and interest. And if you ask what a child remembers about a given class or grade years later, it is likely that it will be something hands-on: the spaceship they built in Grade 5, the model Halifax harbour into which they launched their homemade boats or the giant papier-mâché codfish they created that hung from the ceiling of their classroom.

INTEGRATION OF SUBJECT AREAS

Integration of subject areas is fundamental to most progressive methodologies, although not all. As mentioned at the beginning of this chapter, the core subjects, with the exception of math, are all integrated into theme studies at Halifax Independent School. Science and social studies form the basis for each theme, and teachers are careful to balance the amount of each — some themes lend themselves to an evenly matched approach (boats and shipping, for example) whereas others are almost entirely science or social studies, and must be balanced across themes. Chapter 2 details the opportunities at Halifax Independent School to practise writing for many purposes, as well as the constant reading, skimming and critical thinking involved in doing research. Chapter 3 deals with math, which at Halifax Independent School is taught as a separate subject, although integrated where possible.

There are many opportunities to integrate art into theme studies, as drawing and sketching are ways of recording information, and the Fair presentations may often involve murals, models, sculptures, diagrams, dioramas, videos, posters, paintings and many other artistic representations. Art provides another way for children to express themselves, and it is often used as a lead in or inspiration for writing activities. Music and drama are also frequently integrated as songs and role plays are used to explore different facets of a topic.

Integration works so well because:

1. It is a **natural** way to learn: children learn in a holistic manner, and they are always learning. While reading information about manatees, for example, they are also learning about the structure of a paragraph — the main

idea and supporting arguments. They are learning new vocabulary related to manatees and reinforcing the spelling of basic words. Integration allows them to make the connections, and gain practice with skills while learning content.

2. It provides an **authentic** context for learning the skills we want them to learn: writing a hypothetical thank you letter is not as effective as writing one to someone they have actually met, about something that they have actually experienced (perhaps to a guest speaker). Learning grammar in isolation can be pretty deadly for most children, whereas learning about the importance of tense coordination when writing a speech about ancient Aztec civilizations becomes a necessary step in editing.

3. It allows for a **deeper involvement** in the subject, and therefore more retention: the content matter or topic is being reinforced by the extra reading/writing or art activities. A child who reads about manatees' life cycle once while doing research, and then again in a different passage while doing an exercise about the main idea of a paragraph, will tend to remember more. Alternatively, presenting a main idea exercise — perhaps using a passage that deals with manatees living in a protected area of Guatemala — broadens the children's information base. Making a model based on the research done or writing a creative story set in the historical period studied reinforces both the artistic and content sides of the project.

4. It encourages **emotional involvement** with the topic. A child studying the codfish, for example, may not get excited about the scientific aspect until after they have read a fiction story about a codfish or have made a model of one. Then, they may want to know everything about codfish in order to write a story or to complete a diorama for the model they have made.

In order for true integration to happen, there needs to be long blocks of time set aside for study of the theme or inquiry or topic. At Halifax Independent School, the first hour and a half of the day is simply called "theme," with shorter periods set aside during the rest of the day. Once a week, a whole morning is devoted to "theme" so that classes can go on field trips or do big, messy projects that can't be cleaned up by snack time.

Individual teachers in public schools can integrate their core subjects, but support from administration is needed, or they may find themselves having to justify what they are doing constantly. The ideal is when whole schools decide to adopt integration of the core subjects and the school timetable is designed accordingly. This happens in many alternative and progressive schools, but can happen in public schools with good leadership.

AUTHENTIC SITUATIONS

Providing "authentic," real-life experiences and materials not only helps create a sense of purpose, it allows learning that is deeper, more meaningful and often more memorable than that from secondary sources such as textbooks, educational films or websites.

Frequent field trips are invaluable for deepening a study, and they allow children to experience a place with

Youngs studying airplanes at the aviation museum.

all their senses. When studying water, a class visiting a water filtration plant will have the opportunity to see for themselves where our water comes from. They will see, smell and sometimes feel the processes that water undergoes before being piped to our houses, and they will meet some of the people involved in the work of water. They will have a chance to ask questions whose answers they may have had difficulty finding. They may uncover new areas for research. Field trips may involve extensive planning, or be a simple walk around the block, observing different building styles. Regardless, if a field trip is to be effective, the children must understand the purpose of the trip and have an idea what they would like to learn from it; they must be able to take notes on information that is pertinent to them (having clipboards available is essential), and the follow-up activity will involve incorporating the new information into their research.

Field trips can be used as a catalyst for the introduction of a new topic and give the children some real-life experiences to draw on when doing further research, as well as opening up some avenues for exploration that may not have occurred to them. Conversely, visiting a fish plant in the middle or towards the end of a study of the fishing industry can inject some new excitement or interest into the topic. It also allows students to deepen their knowledge by providing answers to questions such as "What happens to the by-catch?" or "Where do you sell your fish?" — questions they might not have known to ask at the beginning of the study.

Too often field trips are made overly difficult in public schools so that they rarely happen. Encouraging teachers to use public transport or walking means that they are free from having to book an expensive school bus — one Toronto school has "adopted" a nearby ravine where classes can walk easily for frequent nature study. Parents are an invaluable resource, as volunteers and for suggesting or inviting classes to their workplaces — seeing the inside of a postal station was an eye-opener for my students one year, and visiting the labs of various scientist parents can be very exciting!

Inviting guest speakers into the class is another way in which students can learn about their topic directly. Often, guest speakers are drawn from the extended school family or local community, and parents should never be shy about volunteering to come in or making suggestions for good speakers. Many organizations are happy to connect with the community, and universities in particular are very interested in establishing a connection with younger children.

Undertaking real research is exciting and motivating for children. Not only are they discovering something for themselves, they are often quite convinced they are the first to discover it! Real research could include interviewing people (one group of my students each interviewed a person who had immigrated to Canada — their stories became the basis for a book of immigrant stories), doing a survey (our middle school students helped with monitoring sea animals along the coast for a local watershed study) or designing and carrying out original science experiments. Science fairs are excellent venues for students to do original research and are especially good learning experiences when all students participate.

Authentic materials are essential for theme studies and most inquiry-based methods. Textbooks are expensive, restrictive and often contain hidden biases, so they are seldom used; instead, library books, the Internet, literature from organizations, the media and the real world are the sources from which the children get their information. Halifax Independent School spends a relatively small amount of its budget on resources; science equipment, technology and good non-fiction books are a high priority, but generally many of the resources used are free. Children need to know how to learn from real life and from the real experiences that life will bring them.

> **Authentic materials**
>
> My very first teaching position was in Great Whale River (now Kuujjerapik/Whapmagoostui), a remote community in northern Quebec. And my first experience of the importance of authentic materials was early in the school year, when my group of seven-year-old Inuit and Cree children were sitting around a table, each with their shiny new copies of *The Dog Next Door*. Since this was the first year these children had an English teacher without an interpreter, their level of English language was very limited, and most were just starting to learn to read.

The Dog Next Door was an old-fashioned reader, from the Ginn 360 series, published in the 1970s. The children seemed to enjoy the pictures, and loved reading about dogs. I was increasingly uncomfortable with the white suburban lifestyle portrayed; however, materials were limited, and we had been told that this was the reading series used in the school. As a brand new teacher, I didn't dare question it.

On the blackboard behind us were new vocabulary words, each in a colourful cloud. We had read over the words as a group, with the children repeating after me to get the pronunciation right. One of the words was "park." We were taking turns reading from the book, and one child read the selection about going to the park, which was accompanied by a nice picture of a city park with benches, trees and grass. Now these children did not ask many questions, so when one asked, "What is park?" I was thrilled to answer. So I began, "Well, it is a place in the middle of a city . . ." Blank looks. "It is a place where there are benches and grass and trees . . ." More blank looks — to put it in perspective, there was certainly no grass anywhere in Great Whale River, which was on the tree line. Any trees were mostly across the river, and if there was a bench, I don't recall it. At that time, in the mid-1970s, there were not many cars, and roads were rutted tracks. Ski-Doos zoomed anywhere, so the concept of "city" was pretty remote. I don't think they ever really understood what a "park" was — at least, not until they visited a city, years later.

This is when I realized the absolute importance of culturally relevant materials. I ditched the readers, and we started making our own books. I discovered the Creeways series of books and we read all of them (there was no equivalent for the Inuit). I think that is where my theme teaching began — searching for topics that were relevant and interesting to my students. We did a big unit on beavers and I have vivid memories of the huge papier-mâché model beaver dam we made.

ASKING GOOD QUESTIONS

> *"That is the essence of science: ask an impertinent question, and you are on the way to a pertinent answer."*
>
> — *Jacob Bronowski*

Young children are full of questions from the time they can talk. Some ask them non-stop. Children's worldviews are formed from the answers they get to their questions, and, as parents, most of us try very hard to answer them appropriately. We know that our answers need to be tailored to the developmental level of the child, that it is okay to say we don't know the answer and that looking up the answer can spark a shared moment of learning for both parent and child. In a traditional school, however, many children learn that it is the teacher who asks the questions, and the children answer them — and they are often afraid of getting the wrong answer. The longer that kind of passive learning continues, the more their innate ability to frame questions will simply shut down, as children realize that their only job is to fill in or find the predetermined answers to someone else's questions.

Progressive education encourages children to keep asking questions, and helps them become better askers through modelling and practise. Very young children sometimes need help framing questions that will further their research. Older children need guidance to form more penetrating questions that will take their research to a deeper level. Theme or inquiry teaching is a constant encouragement and refinement of this art. Whether it's show-and-tell or a child reading from a favourite book, children are encouraged to ask questions of each other. The teacher (or another student) gives them feedback either directly, by saying, "that's an excellent question" or "can you phrase that a little differently?" or indirectly, by not providing an answer. Then when it is time to delve into a new theme topic, they have had lots of practice, and often are able as a group to come up with a series of good questions, which will form the basis for their research.

The early elementary environment offers more structured question formulation. After a catalyst activity that sparks the children's interest, the class may do a brainstorm with what they know, and what they want to know. The teacher usually writes the class's questions on a chart, which the children can copy into their theme book (leaving lots of space for answers). At the earliest stages (pre-writing), the answers may be found as a class or a small group, and the results written on the chart.

OTHER PROGRESSIVE METHODOLOGIES

Although the Halifax Independent School version of theme studies has some unique characteristics, it shares some commonalities with several other approaches. None of them are concerned with what students can produce on a test, and all aim to produce students who "learn so well that they will learn whatever needs to be learned," who will remember what they have learned and who will enjoy doing it.

The most similar in concept to theme studies is the **inquiry approach,** which has now been adopted by the Alberta Department of Education. It is "a process where students are involved in their learning, formulate questions, investigate widely and then build new understanding, meaning and knowledge."[14] This could easily describe the basic methodology of theme studies, where the students are introduced to a topic, get excited about it, brainstorm to generate questions, research/inquire to find more information and then present their findings in some form (Fair Day). The teacher is a participant in this process (not an expert), and models the behaviour of the inquirer: unexpected events can happen, frustration can result, different sources can say opposing things. The role of meta-cognition, or learning to learn, is central, as reflection about the process is built in.

> **Inquiry-based kindergarten: the Calgary Board of Education**
> My niece has taught for over ten years in Calgary. Vanessa described a "big inquiry" she did with her full-day kindergarten class a few years ago, when she noticed her students were very interested in superheroes. After exploring some comic superheroes, which the children knew about through stories and video, the class talked about the qualities superheroes possessed, and whether they knew any real people who possessed those qualities. They came up with a list of many people in the community they considered heroes, including firefighters, paramedics, police, parents, doctors and teachers. They created illustrated booklets, artwork and dioramas about heroes in the community. And of course there was lots of time provided for dramatic play about superheroes and heroes, with props and costumes to inspire them. A visit from a seeing-eye dog sparked the children's interest in animal heroes. Among other activities, they read stories about animal heroes and animals who had rescued people, and created Lego homes for the animals they were studying. This led to the topic of animal rescue, so the class paid a visit to a local animal shelter.
> The class spent well over a month exploring this inquiry or "theme." She feels that inquiry-based learning is very well accepted and that it works for all children, including those at her "high needs" school.

In the more than ten years since Alberta adopted inquiry-based learning, their scores on international achievement tests have been consistently high, ranking among the top in the world in the PISA studies, and well above the Canadian average on all subjects tested.

Project-based learning (described and developed by Sylvia Chard)[15] involves the students choosing a project to work on based on real-life challenges, and creating, building and testing something that demonstrates their knowledge and that has a purpose beyond the classroom. She describes it as "in-depth learning in which children can take some ownership of their work and through which they have choices that they can make — but choices that are designed together by the child and the teacher." I have worked with students to produce many projects whose purpose was to educate others about various topics: a "claymation" video about four hundred years of Acadian history, board games that deal with the topic of ocean migration or field guides to Nova Scotia birds. For each of these projects, the students had to learn a great deal about the topic, collaborate and share information with each other and then learn about the techniques involved in creating the final product.

Problem-based learning (PBL) (promoted by Sheila Gallagher)[16] begins with a real-life, complex problem being presented to the students. Students are responsible for defining the problem and developing a plan of action, which always involves finding out more information, and the end result is often an action rather than a product. This approach is used today in medical schools and in training other helping professions — where, for example, students are given a set of symptoms for a patient/client and must develop a treatment plan. At Halifax Independent School, some six- and seven-year-olds who were studying the Gully (an ocean area off Sable Island) became concerned about the threats of oil and gas exploration. They developed an action plan that called on the government to make it a Marine Protected Area (MPA). They organized petitions, information booths for Oceans Day and a letter-writing campaign. When the Gully actually was made an MPA a couple of years later, these children felt that it was all their doing.

Design-based learning (DBL) (Doreen Nelson)[17] involves students learning what they need to know in order to design a "never before seen" object. Often used in technology and art education, students plan, experiment with materials, justify their thinking, revise and adjust — all "just in time" to create something new. At Halifax Independent School, students designed and built a playhouse in the early 1980s. Then, upon moving to a new building, the upper elementary children designed and built a very imaginative fort/slide/climbing frame with the help of an architect and other experts.

At Halifax Independent School and most progressive schools, elements of some or all of the above approaches are used, and the different outcomes ensure variety throughout the school year.

COLLABORATION AND LOCAL INITIATIVES LEAD TO PROGRESSIVE CHANGE

One of the most important features of Halifax Independent School is that its curriculum is homegrown, was developed collaboratively and reflects the philosophy of the community of the school and the inclinations of the particular teachers involved. Halifax Independent School's Nova Scotia and Oceans themes reflect the local environment, and allow the use of many local resources. This approach could be used by public schools.

Canada can also learn from Finland. Like Britain, Finland has a national curriculum, but the difference is that the curriculum is described as a "framework" within which schools can include local variations of topics and themes. In addition, teachers' pedagogical autonomy means "they can decide themselves the methods of teaching as well as textbooks and materials."[18]

One of many characteristics that Halifax Independent School shares with Finnish peruskoulu (comprehensive, Grades 1 to 9) schools is the absence of external, standardized assessments. This allows teachers much more freedom to teach how and what they want. Chapter 7 describes in more detail the chilling effect that standardized tests can have on teaching, especially at the elementary level.

Although Finland's decentralized curriculum already encourages integrated study using themes or topics, its next big reform will be to mandate at least one extended period of time in each middle school year in which "phenomenon-based" teaching will happen. All subjects will be integrated into the study of themes such as "the European Union", "Climate Change" or "100 years of Finnish Independence." This reform will ensure that theme-based learning will happen right up to the end of peruskoulu and beyond for all children.

The PISA data shows, among other things, that when teachers and principals can collaboratively and autonomously design their own curricula and assessments at the individual school level, their students do better academically. Finland, Halifax Independent School and many other progressive school systems have dedicated time for this in their yearly and weekly schedules. Countries such as the US and Britain, with their highly standardized exam systems — and low average achievement scores — have ignored these findings.

Fortunately, Canada does not have a national curriculum with all the attendant requirements for delivery and testing as Britain does, and as the US aspires to. Each of Canada's provinces and territories has its own public school curriculum. Nova Scotia, like most provinces, has specific curriculum outcomes for each subject and each grade level, and, while emphasizing the basics, there are opportunities for cross-curricular learning. There are provincial assessments every three or four years up to the end of middle school, but there is not as much at stake on the results, and the curriculum is not as rigidly enforced as in the UK and US. There is more room for schools and teachers to adapt the curriculum to their students' needs.

Many of the provinces have flexibility built in, and there are examples of progressive principles within many school boards, particularly larger urban ones. After its curriculum was overhauled some years ago, Alberta included inquiry-based learning as "not an 'add-on,' but rather a way to achieve the goals of the Alberta programs of study."[19] In Toronto, a group of parents worked together to persuade the school board to open the Equinox Holistic Alternative School, whose philosophy sounds very similar to Halifax Independent's. Opened in 2009, it shares an underutilized building and some specialist teachers with a regular public school. There are some eighteen other elementary/middle schools and twenty-one high schools in the Toronto Board that are described as alternative, each with their own distinct philosophy.

Provincial curricula are flexible enough that the teachers, parents and principal of a school, working together, investing in some planning time and professional development, can change their curriculum to make it more local — perhaps more hands-on or more inquiry-based. There are many examples of schools and communities that have worked together to establish gardens, outdoor classrooms, arts-based programs or health initiatives. A local project to develop a healthy-eating curriculum in the Annapolis Valley started with a group of concerned parents, and has been so successful (at reducing obesity in children, among other things)[20] that it has been shared with other school boards in Nova Scotia.

At a neighbouring public school to Halifax Independent, an enthusiastic parent with a green thumb started a small, school vegetable garden. Over a period of several years, the project grew until the school garden was being used for classroom projects and even some integrated units on food production.

Most schools in Canada have some form of parent advisory groups, whether they are parent-teacher associations, or a committee made up of class parents. Too often these groups deal only with social and/or fundraising issues; however, there is no reason that teachers and parents who wish their children's classrooms to be more hands-on and inquiry-based cannot start tomorrow. Many teachers in public schools receive training in progressive methodologies and feel frustrated when they can't use these techniques in their classes. At Halifax Independent School, parental support for this type of teaching, which is so rewarding for teachers, has been a key ingredient in the development of theme studies. For theme studies and other progressive methodologies to be taken up in public schools, getting parents on board is essential.

Chapter 2
SNEAKING THE LEARNING IN: LITERACY IN AN INTEGRATED ENVIRONMENT

> *"I love this school. Here the teachers sneak the learning in."*
> — *Benazir, five-year-old Halifax Independent School student*[21]

Jeremy was a "free range" eight-year-old child whose only previous experience in formal educational situations had been occasional attendance at a child-care centre with children much younger. He could barely write his own name when he arrived in my class.

He had a copy of *Moby Dick* that he badly wanted to read. I read with him individually during the class silent reading time, starting with easy, predictable books, and helped him learn to print his letters while the rest of the class was practising cursive writing. Beyond that, he got very little extra help at school, although he took lots of books home to read with his mother, as he was so entranced by the idea that he could read by himself.

By December, he was reading and writing at almost a Grade 3 level, and by the end of the school year was reading *Moby Dick* on his own. By Grade 5, his mother was convinced he was gifted because of how quickly he had learned to read and by the quality of his written work. In reality, though, he had been just "itching" to learn to read.

When children start school, parents hope that teachers will recognize their uniqueness. But somehow, that doesn't always happen. Most schools in Canada expect that all six-year-olds are ready to read, and the Grade 1 curriculum is heavily oriented toward teaching reading. In the UK and US, the perceived age for reading readiness is dropping, so that often kindergarten or even preschool is devoted to teaching literacy skills. The danger of pushing literacy on children too early is that it can discourage them — if a child doesn't seem to progress with reading at the age it is being taught, she may pick up on the worry and dismay that the adults around her feel about it. This is unnecessary and damaging for both parents and children.

A traditional school might have forced Jeremy to learn to read before he was ready, and learning to read could have been made into an onerous process. Instead, it was a delight for Jeremy — each new skill he learned made him feel powerful and each book opened up new worlds of knowledge that were previously hidden.

In Finland and other Scandinavian countries, formal school, and therefore the teaching of reading, begins at age seven. Most children in Finland (98 per cent) participate in early childhood education programs, which are play-based and focus on developing social skills, enriching dramatic play and fostering a rich language experience. Formal literacy training is not mentioned as a goal. Nevertheless, "half of the pre-school pupils learn to read as if by chance," says Pirjo Sinko.[22] When children do start primary school, if they haven't already learned, they are "itching" to learn to read. It is significant that Finland, for the past decade, has topped the PISA studies in reading at the age of fifteen, in spite of the later age of formal literacy teaching. Finnish children do not suffer from learning to read later.

Table 1: Comparison of PISA results for reading (mean score)[23]							
2000		2009		2012		2015	
Country	Mean Score	Country	Mean Score	Country	Mean Score	Country	Mean Score
Finland	546	Finland	536	Finland	524	Canada	527
Canada	534	Canada	524	Canada	523	Finland	526
UK	523	US	500	UK	499	UK	498
US	504	UK	494	US	498	US	497
OECD Average	500	OECD Average	493	OECD Average	496	OECD Average	493

How many of us can actually remember learning to read? One children's author, Michael Morpurgo, remembers the "black squiggly lines" magically transforming into words one day when he was reading a book that he had "read" (memorized) many times before.[24] I have a memory of being off school for a couple of weeks with whooping cough when I was six. My teacher sent home my reader and I can still recall the thrill I felt when I opened it and discovered I could read it myself. But Michael and I were lucky — reading came upon us when we were ready, and it felt effortless. Many of us don't remember learning to read, which probably means that it happened at the right time, but for some of us, learning to read was laborious, frustrating and stressful. This is because we were not on the same timetable as other children.

Learning to read should be exciting and enjoyable for both parents and children, and it can and should unfold in an organic, stress-free way. It should allow each child to follow his or her own path. However, standardized methods of teaching reading treat all learners the same, forcing them down a narrow road that misses many interesting, enriching side roads along the way.

Part of the problem is that the ability to read, and read well, has come to represent the base upon which all other academic achievement is built, and it is framed as a predictor of academic success — after all, the exams that measure it are largely reliant on the printed word! It is almost as though educators are convinced that a child cannot learn anything of value until they can read. This fallacy has contributed to the rise of GERM and caused untold frustration and stress for many children and their parents.

The ability to read and write well is certainly very important for many things one wants to do in life; there is no debate about the desirability of producing highly literate students. The issue is the best way of achieving this, and my view is that traditional schooling has put too much emphasis on early reading in the mistaken hope that it will lead to better academic outcomes.

Does it matter to a twenty-five- or thirty-five-year-old if he learned to read at age four, seven or even nine? In my experience, and corroborated by many published studies, there is minimal connection between early literacy and later academic achievement.[25] Yet, in my years as a teacher, I met more parents who were stressed out about their child's literacy progress than about any other educational topic. All too often they seemed to feel their child's entire future hinged on their learning to read early or spell accurately by Grade 3.

> **Elizabeth Abbott, author of *A History of Marriage***
> "I learned to read in Grade 2, after frustrating months of failure. I have a vivid memory of my poor mother chasing after me up the driveway, clutching my hated *Dick and Jane* reader (yes, Virginia, there really were *Dick and Jane* readers) as I escaped on my way-too-big CCM bicycle. And I'd bike up to the shrine, as we

> Anglo-Montrealers called St. Joseph's Oratory, and visit Brother Andre's cottage-cum-museum, which may explain why, toward the end of Grade 2, a miracle! Suddenly I could read, and I haven't stopped since."[26]
>
> A miracle? Certainly, in the sense that each child's entry into the world of literacy is a miracle, but in reality, she describes what happens to every child when they finally are "riding on their own" with reading. Luckily for Elizabeth, she was able to escape the drill and boredom of Dick and Jane by riding away on her bike . . . but she learned anyway. The fact that she was almost eight at the time does not seem to have held her back — she has a PhD in history and is the author of seven books.

THE GREAT DEBATE

After years of work in education, I learned that teaching literacy is more about creating the conditions in which literacy will flourish than about particular methods — but a crucial condition is the readiness (and learning style) of each child.

As part of my training, I had read Piaget and his theory of child development. He identified the stages of development that all normal children go through and, what's more, talked about the futility of trying to teach something to a child that is beyond their developmental level. A child under the age of two, in the sensorimotor stage, thinks that objects just disappear when they are out of sight (which is why playing peek-a-boo with babies is such fun), so you wouldn't try to teach a baby about how trains work. With experience, I saw how children moved through the stages fairly predictably, but each at their own pace. The other lesson I learned from Piaget is that children at all stages are like "little scientists," actively making sense of their environment.[27]

While I was completing my Bachelor of Education program, the field of literacy teaching was in flux. At that time, the whole-language approach, which grew out of constructivist theory, was challenging the phonics-based approach. The phonics method sees reading as a skill that can be broken down into subsets of skills to be taught independently. Children are taught to recognize the smallest chunks (letters and then letter sounds) and are gradually introduced to larger chunks such as blends (*fr*, *str*), digraphs (*th*, *ck*, *sh*) and diphthongs (*ow*, *oy*) in a controlled way until they can decode whole words. There is a progression of skills to be learned, and frequent testing ensures that one set of skills has been mastered before moving on to the next one. Once children learn to decode words, they work on fluency and comprehension. The problem was (and is) that learning phonics in isolation is boring and not developmentally appropriate for many children when it is being taught. Too many children, especially those who came to school already reading, were turned off reading by the drill and repetition that phonics entailed, and many were failing to learn at the age of six when it was typically introduced.

The precursor to Halifax Independent School was at the forefront of the development of the whole-language approach to reading in the 1970s and 1980s, with the input of Judith Newman and others who were active in the field at the time.

Over the past century, these two major approaches have fallen in and out of fashion, and have spawned great debates and research on the merits of the phonics method versus whole language.

The four basic principles of the theory of whole language are:[28]

1. **Humans have an innate need to communicate with each other.** From babbling babies to teenagers on social media, all human beings want to communicate. When children realize that reading and writing is an extension of this basic need, they will want to learn.

2. **Literacy is a way of communicating, in which meaning is constructed (reading) and expressed (writing).** It is not necessary to know all the phonemes/graphemes in order to get the meaning from a text. The reader uses context clues, pictures, prediction, confirmation and a host of other strategies in order to construct meaning. Similarly, these same strategies are used in writing.

3. **Learners should be active participants and use their prior knowledge in order to construct meaning (constructivism) and build on it. They use strategies to ascertain meaning (reading) and express meaning (invented spelling).**

    * Constructing meaning: knowing what a text is about, and being reminded of what they already know, helps readers to construct meaning. They can then fit new words/information in with the old. Beginning readers are shown how to point to words and follow along a predictable text. When they come to an unfamiliar word, they keep going and see if they can guess the unknown word, using pictures and other context clues.

- Constructed spelling: while writing, adults can model saying the words slowly and predicting which sounds to write. Instead of saying "S-P-O-T" when a child asks how to spell the word, the adult will encourage the child to sound it out, helping out by saying "Sss" or "Tuh." Soon the children will be sounding out themselves, gradually adding sounds as they are ready. Constructed or invented spelling is a way to make writing easy so that children will write a lot. This strategy means children take risks; the more they take, the better at predicting and confirming they will become. Feeling safe and confident is of utmost importance. Too much correcting at beginning stages can make children anxious about being wrong and afraid to try out sounds, and thus restrict their writing.

4. **Literacy learning happens best when authentic materials are used, and when purposeful situations demand communication.**

    - Authentic materials are any written materials not produced for the sole purpose of teaching reading (basal readers) and can include storybooks or informational texts written for children, newspapers, lists, letters and brochures. Children are aware of print around them from an early age, and a print-rich environment will encourage them to explore and read more.

> ✻ Children are motivated to learn to read and write when there is a real reason that makes sense to them to do so. Wanting to find out more about an animal that interests them, to read the caption on an intriguing picture or to follow instructions on how to build a model boat are powerful motivators. Making a sign for a lemonade stand or writing a letter to an absent friend encourages writing. Teachers and parents should provide these experiences.

The theme studies approach to education at Halifax Independent School grew out of the fourth principle, that authentic materials and purposeful situations provide the best literacy learning. The two philosophies have become melded together over the years — by integrating literacy into the study of interesting topics, the school ensures that children are becoming literate while they are learning about these topics or themes. The school does not accept the premise that children cannot learn anything worthwhile before they are literate.

> Jojo came to school at the age of five reading simple chapter books fluently. His teacher quickly found out, however, that he was extremely reluctant to try any writing, perhaps because his fine motor skills were very basic. She discovered that he was interested in cars, and gradually steered him into drawing, and then writing about them, initially just using the beginning letters of the makes of cars.
> He was soon holding a pencil properly and learned to form all the letters. By the end of the year, he had moved on to writing whole car names, and eventually sentences about them. Jojo needed help with holding a pencil; he did not need a lot of phonics teaching.

Over the years, research has shown that a certain amount of explicit phonics teaching (as well as the teaching of the mechanics of reading/writing) is very helpful, and that some children need more of it than others. In places where the whole language approach was allowed to develop, as at Halifax Independent, most teachers have integrated phonics and other mechanics into their literacy teaching. This became known as the balanced approach, and the conditions necessary for it to happen include:

1. **Respect the learner as a whole, unique being with emotional, intellectual, physical and spiritual strengths and needs.** Children come to school with a host of experiences, competencies, learning styles and ways of expressing themselves. It is up to the teacher to know and respect all the learners and gear expectations according to each one. This includes discerning their learning style and when they are ready to begin formal reading instruction.

2. **Foster motivation by promoting a love of language, books and learning.** Exposing children to good literature, rich language and a culture of learning from an early age is fundamental to motivating them to become literate. We want them to love books and learning; in order to do this, they must be surrounded by positive role models who read a lot, and they must find learning enjoyable and non-stressful. When children see adults or other children reading, they realize that they have access to knowledge and power, and they want this

for themselves, especially as they get older. Daily stories, book-sharing sessions and silent reading time all promote this.

3. **Learners learn to read and write by doing a lot of it.** Like learning to ride a bicycle or any other skill, practice matters. But practice doesn't have to be boring drill — if students are presented with authentic, purposeful situations in which reading and writing are necessary and pleasurable, they will do a lot of it, and get a lot of practice. The better they get, the more rewarding it is. The more language they are exposed to through reading, the faster their writing improves.

4. **The mechanics of language (phonics, grammar, spelling, punctuation) are presented as a way of making meaning at appropriate times.** Letters, sound-letter correspondences, digraphs and phonemes are introduced to children as they show readiness, but these small parts can also be embedded in meaningful text and pointed out after the fact. If the mechanics of writing are taught as children see the need for them to clarify their writing, children are able to "discover" these mechanics for themselves, rather than having them drilled, and the concepts are absorbed more easily. A child who is writing four-word sentences does not need to know about commas; however, when he starts expressing more complex thoughts and wants to start combining some of those short sentences, the comma will be presented as a useful way of finishing a thought or separating a list.

5. **Literacy is integrated into all aspects of the curriculum.** In a balanced approach classroom, literacy is not confined to one hour of formal teaching per day. It is central to a child's whole experience of school — every situation is a literacy learning opportunity. In order to provide authentic, purposeful literacy experiences, the content needs to be interesting and engaging, and thus the theme approach was developed. The fact that the vocabulary learned is repeated and expanded upon throughout all aspects of the theme gives children ample opportunity to practise discussing, listening, reading and writing.

Over the twenty-plus years I have been associated with Halifax Independent School, the balanced approach has developed in conjunction with the theme approach. It does not shy away from explicitly teaching phonics, or the mechanics of language, but neither does it drill them or adopt a one-size-fits-all strategy for teaching them. Some children will require more concentration on these basics than others, and systematic phonics instruction may be used for those who seem to need more.

LEARNING TO READ STARTS AT BIRTH

Learning to talk and understand speech is an organic process; all children (with few exceptions) learn to talk, almost always without any formal teaching. But in this whole process, certain precursors to talking are necessary — a child needs to be able to physically form the sounds, and differentiate between one sound and another. A babbling baby is in reality practising making sounds, and when responded to (imitation and extension), they will gradually form those

Using many sources for research.

sounds into words and sentences. However, a child who hears nothing but mundane language (or worse, abusive language) will not develop in their listening and speaking as far as one with a rich language environment around them, and one exposed to rich experiences.

> Finn loved playing with the magnetic letters on his fridge, and from the time he was two, he kept asking his parents the names of the letters. By age three, he knew all the letter names and sounds, and soon his parents noticed that he had memorized many of his books. He would "read" them back to them, and before long he could point to the words accurately. Without any explicit teaching, he was able to read unfamiliar books before he turned four.
>
> Finn had all the readiness signs for reading at an early age. His parents recognized them, but did not force him to focus on sounds and letters. They took their cues from him — reading to him as much as before, but allowing him to read aloud as much as he wanted. This was his timetable, and although he is still an avid reader at age nine, many of his peers are equally keen and proficient readers.

Learning to read and write can be an organic process, just like listening and talking. The readiness skills required, besides good speaking and listening skills, are the physical ability to form letters, the ability to see differences in letter shapes and associate them with sounds (this happens at different ages, and may be later in boys) and the concentration required to sit and focus. Children must also have the desire and/or need to learn to read. Seeing others reading around them, at home and at school, and wanting to keep up with them, is a powerful motivator. Also necessary is self-confidence and a feeling of safety, from which children feel they can take on new challenges. The skill in teaching children to read is in recognizing when an individual child has these building blocks of literacy, and understanding the unique manner in which she learns.

Any parent who reads to their young children frequently will relate to how they love to have books read over and over again. Young children will often memorize books, and "read" them back to their parents — this is a vital stage in the reading process. Books with pictures and predictable text that is easy to memorize are extremely important in the early reading stages. "Brown bear, brown bear, what do you see? I see a red bird looking at me. Red bird, red bird, what do you see . . ."[29] and so on, is one of the best known predictable books, and most preschool and early elementary classrooms are full of others. As children progress, they begin to follow along the words with their fingers until one day, the black squiggles form into letters and then words. It is important to remember that there can be years between these stages and actual independent reading. My older daughter could "read" all kinds of books fluently, even sometimes following along with her finger. She knew what text belonged on each

> **Pam's Black Jam**
>
> Pam has a glass.
> The glass has black jam in it.
> Sam pats the glass.
> The glass has a crack.
>
> Sam has black jam,
> and black jam,
> and black jam.

Go Phonics - Level 2 Storybook, 2000, Foundations for Learning.[30]

page. Yet, if I isolated one word on the page such as "the" or "look," she couldn't tell me what it was. This went on for ages and I was starting to worry, until one day, suddenly, she could tell me. I was expecting her to do something that she was just not ready for, but when she was ready she did it and never looked back.

Phonics-based readers use highly controlled vocabulary to reinforce one particular sound, resulting in some fairly stilted, unnatural language. Great literature these books are not, but they may have value for children who require extra help reinforcing language sounds. Most children, however, will find them boring.

While there is no disadvantage in later academic achievement by delaying reading instruction, there are considerable advantages in promoting other kinds of learning between ages five and seven. Imagination, creativity and verbal expression are equally if not more important qualities, and can be crushed if the early years are used to drill the mechanics of literacy through boring repetition and reading stilted children's books. Play, particularly dramatic play, is hugely positive for later academic outcomes. Sara Smilansky defines dramatic play as taking place when a child pretends to be someone else, and socio-dramatic play as when more than one child cooperates in this kind of play. She concludes, "results point to dramatic and socio-dramatic play as a strong medium for the development of cognitive and socio-emotional skills."[31]

THE BALANCED APPROACH TO READING AND THEME STUDIES

During the heyday of whole language theory implementation in the early 1980s, the teachers at Halifax Independent School had the freedom, and the backing of the school's governors, to develop a curriculum based on its principles. Thus, the fifth condition (integrating literacy into the whole curriculum) became the foundation for the theme approach. The two strands, literacy and theme, can complement each other and enable more depth of subject matter as well as more practice of reading and writing by providing authentic, purposeful learning situations all day long. Through having children read and write about interesting topics, which also happen to be related to the social studies or science concepts that would be part of a regular curriculum, teachers really are "sneaking the learning in."

As Gamberg et al say,

> *Practicing reading skills for their own sake can be boring and pointless. One always needs a context to put them in and a purpose for using them — to get information and ideas or for just plain enjoyment. There must be ample opportunity to read for these purposes and a high success rate in these efforts without the constant expectation of perfection.*[32]

Case study: Literacy integrated into a geology theme

On a chilly Monday morning in late November, the fourteen six- and seven-year-old children in Jill's class were divided into three groups. One group went to a table with a box of rock samples and a microscope with samples of sand from beaches all around Nova Scotia, where they were to record what they saw under the microscope. Another group found their journals and began drawing pictures about what they did on the weekend on the blank half of a page. The third group went to a table, the research table, covered with geology books, and got out their "theme" notebooks.

Jill sat down with the group of children at the research table and looked at the questions they had generated about their mineral, coal, in their theme books. Where do we find coal in Nova Scotia? How was it formed? What are the uses of coal? The children took turns reading what they had already written, and decided to look for uses of coal in the picture books they had. Jill helped them read a few paragraphs, and then asked them to tell her if it had answered one of their questions.

"Yes, we use coal for steam engines!" said Ben.

"And what else?" she prompted.

"Power plants!" interjected Charlie excitedly.

They had a little chat about the power plants that produced electricity for all our houses. The children then wrote down in their own words (and creative spelling) a sentence about the uses of coal. Using the books as sources, the children answered all their questions. They had a blank page labelled "interesting facts," so Jill asked them what else they knew about coal that they found interesting. Charlie said, "My dad told me diamonds are made from coal."

"Wow, that's interesting," she said. "Let's see if we can find out something about that on the computer." She knew they were keen to look on the computer for more information. So they looked up "coal into diamonds," and found that it is a myth; in fact, diamonds

> were formed billions of years ago, many eons before coal was formed. Charlie was shocked and insisted they look on another website, because it was his dad who had told him. They did, and it corroborated the first website. Jill told them that many people thought that diamonds came from coal (she had thought that herself) and would be very surprised to find out it wasn't true. Charlie in particular was very excited about debunking this myth at the Fair!
>
> Jill moved to the journal group, who were just getting started on writing a sentence or two about the picture they had drawn. Jenny dictated her sentence to Jill, who wrote it on a piece of scrap paper so that Jenny could copy it into her journal. Eva read her sentences to Jill: "On the weknd i saw a moovee it was frzn. Anna savd Elsa the qeen.It was vry cold." Jill suggested that there needed to be one more period there, and Eva quickly found where to put it and capitalized the following "I." After checking in with the rest of the group, Jill took a second group to the research table, and the other groups switched activities.

The theme studies approach, based on whole language principles, aims to produce learners who maintain a sense of wonder and at the same time are learning solid literacy skills. This process takes time; indeed, it is the goal of any primary education system. In practical terms, it means that teachers take their cues from the children as to when to start formal reading instruction; they do not force them to focus on the printed word before they are ready. In the case study above, Jill did not correct the children's spelling in their journals, but noted that Eva was already using periods, and judged that she was ready to add one in order to clarify the meaning. There is a fine line to walk: too much correcting might inhibit her desire to write or at least try new words, but pointing out ways to make it easier to read (such as adding periods) helps her move on in her reading and writing. Jenny, on the other hand, was just beginning to form letters, and needed encouragement to get them down on paper, so Jill allowed her to copy her sentence. Small classes enable the teacher to pay attention to the uniqueness of each child and judge when they are ready for the next stage of literacy learning.

Many authors who analyze the teaching of reading and writing cite examples of how the deepest learning happens at a time when the learners are really engaged in the subject matter. Jennifer Story describes a group of boys, calling themselves the "yoyomen," who collaboratively wrote a book to share yoyo techniques:

> *Writing a book of yoyo tricks was meaningful and useful to these boys. In incidental fashion, they were learning the academic subjects of spelling, grammar, punctuation, organization, and coherent writing. The learning was effortless to them and continual. The learning was also collaborative, as each boy brought a different world of knowledge and expertise to the task.*[33]

These authors often bemoan the fact that this type of learning happens so rarely in schools where the day is chopped up into different subject areas. Theme studies, however, allows this type of learning to happen all the time.

Children are closely observed and encouraged in literacy-related activities. The children who have absolutely no interest in the written word will have more opportunity to play in an unstructured way, and may spend their journal time drawing and describing verbally what they are drawing until they show readiness. Some may dictate the details of their picture to the teacher while others may write a description in their own invented spelling. Seeing other children writing is a powerful motivator and often will inspire children to attempt writing on their own, even if it is just "pretend writing."

In the early elementary years, phonics is "embedded" within the theme activities. While doing a shared writing activity with the whole class or a small group, the teacher may think out loud as she is writing, sounding out words and pointing out interesting patterns. Punctuation, capitalization and sentence formation are all introduced, and lively discussions about the placement of "the period" may take place. Journal writing is an important part of the day, when children apply what they know about phonics to write about a picture they have drawn, and it is fascinating to watch a child's "invented" spelling develop over the years and converge on conventional spelling. Individual conferencing and small group work enable a teacher to observe, work on appropriate skills and challenge the children to extend their learning.

By the time a child is eight or nine, and reading short chapter books on their own, formal spelling practice can be introduced. This brings children's attention to the structure of words, and the myriad spelling patterns and exceptions that make up the English language. By the end of two years of formal spelling, some children may be spelling virtually conventionally; these children will be moving on to more intense vocabulary study, looking at the etymology of words as well as words of increasing complexity. Others will continue with spelling practice until they are deemed to be conventional spellers, generally by the end of elementary school.

Sharing a book with a friend.

The balanced approach promotes a love of literature for its own sake by frequent reading aloud of well-crafted books and silent reading time (sometimes called DEAR, "drop everything and read", time or SSR, sustained silent reading). Most schools have a "book buddy" program, where younger children pair with older ones for a half hour of shared weekly reading. They are encouraged to take turns reading to each other, and older children are given basic instruction in how to help the younger ones (e.g., point to the words, look at picture cues to predict meaning, don't insist on laborious sounding out). Teachers encourage literature extension activities, in which children discuss and do an activity based on a story or book that they have read, often creating a display of pictures. Home reading programs, where children take books home to share or read independently, also foster a love of reading and literature in the elementary years. Creative writing for its own sake is encouraged as children read more widely.

As the children progress through elementary school, the learning process focuses less on hands-on activities and more on learning and researching from other sources, largely the printed word. They are expected to write more as they are capable, and to write in a way that is clear and legible. In addition to formal spelling, grammar and other language mechanics are introduced in a systematic manner, all in the context of communicating clearly. As with spelling, children practise writing skills through researching theme-related topics and producing little books or other forms of reporting. They reread their rough copy, adding punctuation, circling and correcting spelling mistakes and checking to clarify meaning. Their ability to edit their own work grows as they do.

The end of elementary school focuses on developing and extending independence in writing and researching. Considerable attention is paid to the editing process — not just for grammar, spelling and punctuation, but also for organization, voice, vocabulary and originality.

In all the multi-age classes at Halifax Independent School, the range of literacy levels is wide, although it narrows as children get older. While doing theme research, some children may be capable of reading and extracting information from factual texts at a grade level well above their own. Some younger children may be looking at theme-related picture books, and dictating information to a teacher that they will later copy. The teachers also take research information from books and help students interpret it, either by reading with them or giving them simplified versions. However, all the students will be contributing to class brainstorming sessions and discussions about the theme. They will all produce the same type of project (whether it be a model, a play, a radio show or a booklet); the difference will be in the amount and level of written work. They will all make a presentation at Fair Day, and will be an "expert" in their subject, ready to answer questions from the audience. They feel competent, regardless of their reading level, because the teachers have created a positive atmosphere in which the children discover reading as they are ready.

Just as parents can encourage a child to talk and listen by providing a language-rich environment and lots of one-on-one interaction, so schools can provide a literacy-rich environment. But most parents do not sit their children down and tell them that now is the time to learn talking. Why then are some schools so rigid about teaching reading?

PLAYWRITING: WRITING COLLABORATIVELY FOR A PURPOSE

One year, the school theme was Oceans and my eight- and nine-year-olds had been studying the Gully. The children had learned how this Marine Protected Area off Sable Island had been threatened by oil and natural gas exploration, as well as by fishing trawlers and draggers, and they were very concerned about its preservation.

Playwriting is a major creative writing focus for the upper elementary classes for a term, and it's a collaborative effort. These plays will be performed as part of the annual "Plays" unit, a two to three week all-school integrated effort. The children are highly invested in producing an entertaining, fun-to-perform play in which the other children will enjoy participating. It is a "purposeful situation" that provides a real-life context for the children's writing. They are adapting/writing something in dramatic form, and have to pay attention to scene changes, stage directions and character development. They also have to create enough roles of varying complexity to match the ages and numbers of children involved — from choral speaking roles for the youngest to more meaty ones for the eldest students. There's nothing like knowing that your play will be performed in front of a real audience to focus your attention!

Given the children's interest in the environmental threats to the Gully, I thought that Dr. Seuss's *The Lorax*, a classic tale of environmental destruction and hope, might capture their imaginations. In this story, the Lorax tells the tale of the destruction of the truffula trees, and all the creatures dependent on them, when someone gets the bright idea to make "thneeds (which everyone needs)" out of them. Soon, the thneed factory pollutes and uses up all of the resources, pushing out all the creatures dependent on them. The children had already written adventure stories starring the Gully creatures they had studied, so there was a cast of characters already set to go. After discussing the themes and lessons of *The Lorax* (greed, environmental destruction, redemption, rebuilding), the class easily agreed that they could be the basis for a story about the Gully; ideas for ways to adapt them poured out, and I had to write fast to get them all down in the brainstorm. I asked the children to think more about some ideas for the play, and the next morning, we focused our brainstorming to come up with a detailed outline.

We started by identifying the way the story would be told (for example, who would be the Lorax character?) and then we collectively wrote our own outline on chart paper. Once we had the outline, we brainstormed the characters needed for each scene, making sure to include a sufficient number, and dividing them into small, medium and large speaking parts. We chose a group role for the four-year-olds; this time they would be a school of baby codfish who would be learning how to swim together with their teacher, Miss Cheek. We also identified elements of the original story that we wanted to incorporate into the play, including several poetic refrains such as, "I am the Lorax who speaks for the trees, which you seem to be chopping as fast as you please", and "But I had to grow bigger. So bigger I got. I biggered my factory. I biggered my roads. I biggered my wagons. I biggered the loads . . ."[34]

The children decided on two narrators to take on the role of the Lorax character. The first, Captain Agnes, had started out fishing with her father in a small boat, but had, over the years, increased the size and sophistication of her trawler until she was threatening both the corals and the codfish stocks. The second narrator, Dr. Handsome Flyers (loosely based on Dalhousie oceanographer Ransome Myers, with whose work the children were familiar) would draw out the story and eventually "save the day." This discussion and brainstorming time is exceedingly important, and it took at least two sessions — it is vital that all children participate, and feel part of the effort, so it is worthwhile stopping the discussion if they appear tired or distracted. Often, coming back to it the next day results in some new inspiration, as the children have had time to digest and talk among themselves.

Finally, it was time to get down to the business of writing. The class was divided into groups, and each group given a scene to write. They were given a large sheet of paper and markers, and instructed to share the roles of "scribe" and "discussion leader." Naming the characters often generates lots of discussion and giggling, as does deciding how to translate the action into play dialogue. The naming of characters is a crucial stage, as it often brings the characters alive to the

SNEAKING THE LEARNING IN: LITERACY IN AN INTEGRATED ENVIRONMENT

First reading of the play.

children, and allows some of the quieter ones to feel that their contributions are valuable. In this case, we had ready-made characters from the children's previous stories, but generally, this stage takes time. Choosing a good writer as the first scribe helps to focus attention and get the writing started. Once a few lines are written down, the dialogue tends to flow more easily. During this stage, the children are usually sprawled on the floor either in the classroom or in the hall — keeping space between the groups helps concentration. After a period of focused writing (the time will depend on the class), we would "check in" with the whole group, and some groups, perhaps a little further on in the process, would share what they had written so far. This inspired other groups, which may have been having difficulty getting started, and often ideas for continuity would come up during this sharing.

It may take several sessions of cooperative writing to finish up the scenes. During these sessions, I would be encouraging, offering the occasional suggestion if a group was truly stuck, helping to fact check and ensuring that conversations were on track. Frequent check-ins ensure that there are no overlaps, and that character development is consistent. When all the groups were finished, I collected the papers and took on the job of typing up the whole play. During this process, there were some "enhancements" made, some inconsistencies ironed out, and some rough areas smoothed over; if I had to substantially change anything, I would consult with the authors of that scene. This part took several days as it had to be done in the evenings, but there was always great excitement when I had a typed version to share with the class. Then we read the whole play aloud, taking parts, and made any corrections that had to be made. Now the play was ready to share!

> **Excerpt from the Gullorax:**
> *Captain Agnes and fishers in a boat. Enter Lightbob, (anglerfish) swimming.*
> **Lightbob:** I am Lightbob, I speak for the creatures, the creatures so deep. So stop overfishing on the Gully slopes steep! Your nets are so wide and so big and so tall, no creatures can escape them, no creatures at all!
> **Captain Agnes:** What is this? Look at these poor fishers! If I don't give them jobs, who will? Besides, I am saving all my money to buy an even bigger boat. Then we'll really be able to catch fish!
> **Fisher Megan:** We need more and more fish! We have families to worry about too, you know!
> **Fisher Stephanie:** And with a bigger boat we won't have to work as hard and we can catch even more fish.
> **Fisher Mary:** Then we can buy more and more stuff.
> **Fisher Blade:** And all that stuff will never be enough.
> **Fisher Fred:** And you'll continue to be in a huff!
> **Captain Agnes:** I'm going to bigger my boat, I'm going to bigger my trawl, I'm going to bigger my crew, I'm going to bigger my haul!

HOW GERM HAS INFLUENCED LITERACY TEACHING

After all these years, one would hope that the balanced approach would have put the whole language versus phonics debate to rest. Generally, most Canadian schools use a blend of the two. On a continuum from drilling phonics to unschooling, where children teach themselves, Canada's approach to reading is somewhere in the middle.

However, the "back to basics" movement has failed to recognize the melding of the phonics and whole-language approaches, and it chooses to blame whole language for the perceived lack of literacy skills. This is based on the fear that with whole language, children are somehow not learning basic linguistic structure. It is easy and misleading to look at a seven-year-old's invented spelling in isolation and conclude that she is not learning to spell, simply because this type of organic learning is not easy to capture on a single-year test; however, when one sees the progression of a child's spelling over several years, the acquisition of spelling rules is evident. A good balanced-approach teacher will observe the stages of spelling, and measure progress in terms of these stages.

For example, a beginner might write: "ystday mi fs did". Later: "ystrday my fsh dide". Still later: "yestrday my fish died". And finally, at anywhere from eight to eleven years of age, most children will be able to spell most words conventionally.

Similarly, children learning with a balanced approach who are presented with words in isolation on a vocabulary test may not be able to identify them, whereas if they see them in context in a passage or story book, they may be able to "guess" what they are. Conventional literacy testing at early ages is unreliable and misleading.

Sadly, Britain and the US have moved closer to the drill end of the continuum, and "systematic phonics" is now taught to five-year-olds. In commenting on the British National Literacy Strategy, the Association of Teachers and Lecturers stated: "the consequent marginalisation of speaking and listening has had perverse consequences in terms of exciting children's interest in language and literature. Even more importantly, children need to talk and to experience a rich diet of spoken language, in order to think and learn . . . talk is 'arguably the true foundation of learning'." The Early Childhood Foundation agreed: "Phonics teaching is not appropriate for children in pre-school or reception [kindergarten] classes . . . presented with material which is out of context or uninteresting, children may well repeat sounds or words by rote, but not assimilate these into their knowledge base."[35]

In the US, the National Reading Panel (NRP) was appointed by Congress in 1997 to do a meta-analysis of educational studies on reading since 1960 to identify best practices in the teaching of reading. The NRP based their research on their model of a "hierarchy of skills" in reading, the most important of which were decoding (phonemic awareness), fluency and comprehension.[36] The studies showed that systematic phonics instruction improved reading outcomes; the report lauded phonics-based methodologies and was used as the basis for "Reading First," a component of the No Child Left Behind initiative.

One dissenter on the panel, Dr. Joanne Yatvin[37], wrote a minority report criticizing both the methodology and the composition of the panel. There have since been many more critiques, focusing on the lack of impartiality, flawed methodology and misinformation presented in the summarized version, which was the version sent to all schools.[38]

British and American schools ignore the uniqueness of each child, and their differing developmental levels. GERM says it is more efficient to teach the same thing to everyone at the same time, but as Table 1 shows, it does not produce better results by the age of fifteen. The balanced approach to reading recognizes when children are ready and teaches them what they need, when they need it. Since a class with everyone at different reading levels means small classes are essential, it may be more costly in the early years. But I question the efficiency of a system in which an ever-growing proportion of children are diagnosed with a reading "disability" because they are not reading fluently at the age of eight.

The corollary of the assumption that all children should be reading fluently by age seven is that if a child hasn't become a fluent reader by this age, there is something wrong: he is not trying hard enough, the teaching is ineffective or the child is labelled as having a disability. Often the response to this is to push children more, give them more work to do (phonics exercise books are a popular choice) and exhort them to work harder. All of these responses are counterproductive if children are not ready because they do not have the aforementioned building blocks of literacy. Pushing a child too early can have lasting effects on self-confidence, motivation to read (and indeed, to come to school) and adult-child relationships. Worse, some children respond to force by rebelling completely, and what parent wants their child to hate books and reading? Sadly, I have seen many children in conventional schools who start out at school at age five full of excitement, but who, after a year or two, need to be dragged there. In Britain, the high truancy rate speaks volumes about the disaffection of a large number of students.

DYSLEXIA, DISABILITY, DISORDER — DISASTER?

> Sarah was a lively, active little girl who started Halifax Independent School at the age of five. She was athletic, artistic and a natural leader with a good imagination. She had difficulty concentrating in school, and did not seem interested in learning to read for a few years. Later, as she observed the other children writing more, she began emulating them, and produced reams of almost illegible printing, beautifully illustrated.
>
> At the age of eight, when she did not seem to "take off" with her reading as expected, in spite of her desire to read and individual reading help, she was referred for testing and was found to have a moderately severe phonological awareness disorder. Several years of outside school help resulted, and she eventually learned to read, but never found academic work easy. In spite of all this, she continued to be a leader among her peers, finished high school with honours, went to university and graduated with a degree in drama.
>
> Her confidence, self-esteem, faith in herself and ability to work hard continued in spite of all the setbacks. And throughout her time at Halifax Independent School, she was never identified by her peers or other parents as a child with special needs — indeed, she excelled in group work and in the presentation aspect of the program. She was happy, and did not let her literacy difficulties damage her academic life.

In my early career, I heard many references to dyslexia, usually about children who were struggling to read in the middle elementary grades. Dyslexic children were often described as children who couldn't read because somehow they saw letters backwards, and samples of mirror image printing were given as evidence of the condition. As I gained more experience with readers, I kept looking for a good definition of dyslexia, feeling that once I had that, I could learn how to address it. But it wasn't until I was teaching in England in 2001, where the word was being used all the time, that I finally asked the resource teacher what they actually meant by the term. The answer I got? "It's just a child that can't read." At that point I realized how little we knew about the process of reading.

> Jordan was going through a difficult time at home, with an alcoholic father and a mother desperately trying to leave her marriage. He was a big boy for eight and angry a lot of the time, particularly so when he had to spend his Literacy Hour with my group of "Least Able" children. He considered himself a good reader, and resented being helped. He was a good decoder, and found the phonics exercises we did insulting. Often, however, he missed the meaning of passages he read because of misinterpreting a few key words. When he made a mistake on a comprehension question, he would often pick an argument with Peter, who was always trying to antagonize him. Jordan had already been "excluded" from school for several days at a time for fighting, and I worried that as he grew older this pattern would become habitual. It was very difficult for me to give him the help he needed in that group, where many of the children needed a focus on phonics.

Many bright children in Britain have been streamed into special programs because they haven't learned to read when expected to. The children I taught there were already labelled "Least Able" at eight years old because they had "failed" the reading portion of the scholastic achievement test they had taken at the age of seven. They spent their "Literacy Hour" every day with me so that they could work on their reading and writing skills. But eight of the twelve children in the group were quite normal children, who definitely felt resentful about being taken out of their regular class and were beginning to feel that school didn't matter to them. Did they have a disability because they couldn't read? I didn't think so — it was at this point that I began to question the whole idea of a reading disability. The eight "normal" children in the class were progressing, and I wasn't doing anything with them that I wouldn't do with any other child.

I realized that there was no magic bullet for reading "problems," and that many children who were labelled with a reading disability or dyslexia were actually just late bloomers. Some of my students needed to be re-taught the basic sounds of language, because they had not been ready when they were taught the first time. Some just needed more one-on-one reading time — they may have come from homes where reading was not a priority. Some had language difficulties, which required some speech therapy, or which they outgrew on their own. And there were a few, like Jordan, who had emotional problems stemming from their family situations. Most of the late readers that I encountered did not need a lot of extra help, but they each needed something different and the Literacy Hour couldn't provide that for all of them. It is no wonder that in 2006, only 40 per cent of British children reported reading for pleasure.[39] I suspect that many of the students I taught left school early and joined the legions that swell Britain's high drop-out contingent.

There are children who have difficulties that require more intensive help for reading that is beyond what a classroom teacher can do, but these are a tiny proportion. The need for additional assistance should be very rare, unless a school uses a one-size-fits-all method of teaching that doesn't recognize differences in development. Then there may be a significant number who don't get what they need at the right time, and end up being labelled with a disability — the number of children on "individual program plans" or the equivalent in public schools is a testament to this.

Of greater concern are children who come from homes where literacy is not a priority, where parents do not read or where language is limited, perhaps because another dialect or language is spoken in the home. In these cases, children may have missed out on the preschool years of learning about the English language, including developing their phonological awareness, learning to listen and speak and learning about books and writing. This is where universal early childhood education becomes essential; if every Canadian child had access to a literacy-rich early childhood program from the age of three, there would be fewer children with reading difficulties in elementary school and perhaps higher academic achievement later on. Research, including from PISA, points to a direct correlation between years of early childhood education and academic achievement.

I have seen parents twist themselves into knots because their children were not reading at the normal time. Tutoring agencies benefit enormously from parents' fear that their child has a learning disability that must be tackled early if the child is to be successful. I feel sad when I see six-year-olds marched off to after-school tutoring because they are behind in reading, thus interfering with their playtime, whittling away their self-esteem and contributing to school anxiety. What I do know is that it is unnecessary and contributes to parents' fears. It is no coincidence that the increase in early reading teaching and testing has resulted in a windfall for private tutoring companies.[40]

LITERACY AND THE HOME/SCHOOL CONNECTION

Loving reading and loving learning go hand in hand, and children's entry into the world of literacy is one of the crucial turning points in their lives. A literacy-rich home environment is important, but having one at school is also vital, especially for those children who haven't come from homes where literacy is a priority. Although most Canadian public schools use the balanced approach to teaching literacy, an increased reliance on standardized testing adds pressure on teachers to resort to drilling the basic skills in order to increase test scores. If this happens, it will drain the joy out of learning to read and write. The "miracle" of learning to read may become (and already has become, for many) an anxiety-laden chore that can threaten learning for life.

At Halifax Independent School, in the early years there is almost daily contact between teachers and parents, and much of the conversation is around books and reading. Books appropriate for each child's reading level travel back and forth between home and school, and parents and teachers trade insights on children's progress. There is usually at least one meeting each year focused on how the school teaches literacy, and giving parents tips on how they can support their children's emerging literacy at home. Teachers encourage parents' input to ensure that each child remains motivated, enthusiastic and confident about their reading.

Some things that parents/caregivers of new and developing readers should consider include:

- Reading aloud together needs to be an enjoyable bonding activity between parents and children, and it can continue as long as it stays like that. I have known families that still read aloud with almost-teenagers!

- It is not a time for correction or coercion; indeed, the teacher should know if reading becomes a struggle.

- Parents should read predictable and other books aloud as long as the child needs them to. As they memorize predictable books, children can gradually take over. As they get more fluent, parents can encourage them to follow along with a finger.

- Even when a child seems to be reading fluently, it is okay, as they read longer books, for the parent to "share" the reading, sometimes reading alternate pages.

- When helping children's initial writing efforts, it is important to encourage them to sound out words themselves. Telling them the letters is not as effective as modelling sounding out.

- Do not insist upon correct spelling in the early stages. Indeed, correcting too many errors can result in children being unwilling to take risks or even to write.

- The teacher is a partner in the process, and can help the parent recognize the next stages in a child's literacy progress: when to expect the child to include vowels in his writing, when he should understand some basic spelling rules or when she should be spelling conventionally.

- When your child asks for help editing a piece of writing, ask her to self-edit first (circle spelling and grammar errors that they can see), and then read the piece through with them. At this stage, you can point out corrections that they have missed. *Never* sit down with a pencil and circle mistakes without the child present.

- It is important, especially at the beginning stages, that children learn to bond with books, not just computer screens. The array of computer programs and games promising to improve literacy skills is tempting, but we are starting to hear about many negative long-term effects of screen time on very young children.[41]

The balanced approach to literacy has continued to evolve over the years, even as many other school systems have gone further down the road toward drilling phonics at ever-younger ages. The key to good literacy teaching is knowing when children are ready to move on to the next stage of acquiring literacy skills, and integrating literacy into the other areas of the curriculum. But it is also nurturing the joy children get out of discovering the written language. When teachers consciously structure situations that allow children to be intensely absorbed in something they are really interested in while learning literacy skills, the children may think that the school is just "sneaking the learning in." This certainly does not happen by chance, and it works much better than hammering away at drills.

Chapter 3
FIGURING IT OUT: HANDS-ON MATHEMATICS

> *"I'm sure I'd get on better with geometry if only he wouldn't change the letters,"* complained Anne. *"I learn the proposition off by heart and then he draws it on the blackboard and puts different letters from what are in the book and I get all mixed up. I don't think a teacher should take such a mean advantage, do you?"*
> — L.M. Montgomery, Anne of Green Gables

Many of us can relate to Anne's dilemma. It is pretty typical of what happens when children learn math by rote, without understanding what they have learned. Fortunately we now know how to teach math in ways that allow children to develop a deeper understanding of concepts — I call it hands-on math, and Halifax Independent School has been doing it for forty years.

> A group of eight- and nine-year-olds are working on the floor with brightly coloured geometric shapes called pattern blocks. The teacher explains their task, modelling a few examples. "Write as many equations as you can think of that show the relationships between the blocks. For example, how many blue blocks will exactly cover a yellow block?" They can see that it is three.
> "So, what is the relationship between the yellow and blue blocks?"

One child answers, "One yellow equals three blue blocks." The teacher writes this on the board. "Great, now can anyone think of a different way we can write the same relationship?" Silence ensues. "Well, how about this: what is one blue block equal to?"

"Ahhh . . ." A group of hands shoots up. "One blue block equals one third of a yellow block?" The children get their notebooks and get to work.

Jenna has put two yellow hexagons together, and covered them with green triangles. "Look at this!" she says to the group, "Two yellows equals twelve greens."

"What's another way you can say that?" asks the teacher. Jenna thinks for a moment.

"I guess . . ." she says slowly, "I could say that one green equals one twelfth of two yellows." She moves the yellow blocks apart. "But really, it is still the same as before, one green equals one sixth of one yellow."

"Hey, I already got that one!" chimes in Josh excitedly.

"Some really good problem solving going on over here!" says the teacher.

Exploring fractions with pattern blocks.

In math classes like this one at Halifax Independent School, students are chatting, moving about the classroom measuring furniture, sprawling on the floor and arranging blocks, drawing elaborate designs on grid paper, filling in charts with numbers or writing math stories in their notebooks. I marvel at the contrast with the way I was taught. These children are having fun and learning by experiencing the relationships between fractions. They are discovering the concept of equivalent fractions by actually arranging colourful shapes they can both feel and see. This hands-on activity allows the children to develop the deeper understanding they will need to build on as they progress to more difficult concepts.

In the classrooms of my childhood, the apex of success for a teacher was hearing a pin drop as all thirty-five of us worked diligently away at the same sheets of math questions. The teacher told us how to do the questions, and our job was to memorize the method and the math facts. A few of us may have understood what we were doing, but I don't remember anyone enjoying math class much.

After a fling with "new math" in the 1960s, most schools in North America went back to teaching math the traditional way, with rote learning of facts, memorizing algorithms and solving artificial problems. But by 1983, educators in the US were seeing declining math achievement. They began to look for ways to bring more understanding of concepts into the teaching of math. The US National Council of Teachers of Mathematics developed a series of standards, based on the principle that reasoning and problem solving should be the basis for math teaching rather than rote learning. Students need to "understand abstract and difficult mathematical ideas, see relevance in the mathematics they are learning, and achieve mathematical competence."[42]

Hands-on math is in tune with the Halifax Independent School's child-centred philosophy that young children learn best through doing. It "is rooted in real life situations with an emphasis on seeing patterns and relationships inherent in the world around us." Math is "a hands-on, creative activity focusing on developing conceptual understanding, solving problems and articulating solutions, while providing ample opportunity for practice."[43] There are legions of academic studies that show that using manipulatives — concrete materials that allow children to see and feel mathematical relationships — and other hands-on methodologies helps student learning.[44] In a Halifax Independent School classroom, children are introduced to new concepts with free and guided exploration of manipulatives and with real-life examples. These are the building blocks for both mathematical literacy and, ultimately, the ability to work at the symbolic level. The manipulatives are attractive, and handling them can seem like playing to children — even when they are working on challenging problems. In the case study above, Jenna is uncovering relationships between fractions greater than one — improper fractions, which are often not introduced until much later. She is recording her findings, and will be excited to share them with the whole group later.

Keeping children engaged and interested regardless of their learning styles or developmental stage is important to the success of hands-on math. As they progress, children rely less and less on the manipulatives and more on mental math. Like training wheels on bicycles, eventually the manipulatives get in the way, slow children down and are jettisoned. Even at upper levels, however, they are useful to introduce new concepts. The key to hands-on math is that it emphasizes understanding and problem solving over drill and memorization.

In the public school systems, most provinces have adopted more hands-on math teaching over the years. By 2010, most provinces had overhauled their math curricula and developed texts and resources to support the new approach.

CONCEPTS AND STRATEGIES

Place value is a fundamental mathematical concept underlying all others; children need to know this concept before they can move on to working with larger numbers. Having a good understanding of place value is also a practical skill to have, especially when making change or knowing the difference between a $1,000,000 cheque and a $100,000 one. Understanding decimals or scientific notation also needs a good grounding in place value. Children who are not given the time they need to fully master this and other "building block" notions will struggle with later concepts.

> Base 10 blocks are another manipulative children love to play with, and are excellent for helping them really understand place value as well as concepts that are built on it. A group of seven-year-olds is ready to learn about making exchanges (carrying) when adding two-digit numbers. The blocks are centimetre cubes ("units"), 10 x 1 centimetre "rods" and 10 x 10 x 1 centimetre "flats," which represent ones, tens and hundreds.
>
> These children are only using the units and rods, and have laminated mats on which they display their work. Their job is to model a series of addition equations, draw them on their sheets and solve them. The first equation is 42 + 31. One child counts out four rods and two units, and puts them in the appropriate place on the mat. The next child does the same with 31. Another child combines the units and the rods, and together they count the units first and then the rods. They all draw the rods on their sheets (using a stick to represent a rod and a small square to represent a unit) and put the answer in the blank. This is repeated for the next four examples on the sheet. The teacher notices that some children are drawing the rods and units on the sheet, and finding the answer before the real ones are counted.

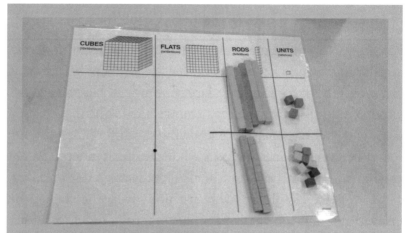

Adding with base ten rods.

The sixth question causes a stir: 53 + 28. Many of the children want to write the answer as 711. One child says, "No, that's 7 hundred and 11. That doesn't make sense." Another child, who has come across this type of problem before, suggests taking the 11 units and exchanging it with 1 rod and 1 unit, and then adding the rods and the units to get 81.

$$53 + 28 =$$
$$50 + 3 + 20 + 8$$
$$50 + 20 + 11$$
$$50 + 20 + (10 + 1) = 81$$

Adding horizontally — grouping tens and ones.

The teacher models writing the problem on the white board, and asks for suggestions as to how to record the exchange that has just happened. The group decides to circle the 10 units that have been

> exchanged and put an arrow over to the tens column. One child insists on putting an X over the units that have been exchanged so she doesn't get confused. Another child suggests a different strategy for recording the sum. They get to work on several more examples, each using their own strategy.

It is true that a child can be taught to add 53 + 28 by adding 3 + 8 and then adding 5 + 2 (+1 that is carried over) without having any real understanding of place value. The "traditional math" folks would say that as long as they know the algorithm, that is all they need (even though a calculator can perform the same operation much quicker, as they will soon discover).

But learning to add two-digit numbers by first playing with piles of Base 10 blocks, grouping them into tens and ones, exchanging the thirteen ones with one ten rod and three ones reinforces the concept of place value as well as addition. Presenting the addition problem horizontally (53 + 28 =) supports the idea that an exchange is happening, and requires the learner to actively identify the ones and the tens instead of simply "adding the right-hand column, carrying, then adding the left." Children who practise using this horizontal method may not do as many sums as a child using the conventional method in a class, but they are using higher order thinking skills and opening themselves up to "light bulb" moments. Once they are comfortable with two-digit addition, they will move on to adding into the hundreds and thousands, and a similar process can be followed introducing "flats" (hundreds) into the Base 10 rods and then "blocks" (thousands). It does become more cumbersome at this point, so when she is sure that a child understands the concept, the teacher can introduce a "shortcut" and the child takes great pleasure in learning the conventional algorithm of adding vertically. But it is important to note that all these ways of adding are considered strategies, and children are encouraged to invent their own strategies, share them with others and find the one that they are most comfortable with. In doing so, they are experiencing the creative aspect of math.

Of course, children need to not only understand the basic concepts, but to know the math facts as well. As they reach the end of a hands-on elementary math program, their grasp of the basic skills has been reinforced by constant practice in different problem-solving situations, quizzes and games. At Halifax Independent School, it is expected that students will have mastered their multiplication tables up to twelve by the end of Grade 6. The difference is that they will have done it not because the teacher says they must do so, but with the knowledge that multiplication facts will be helpful in many real-life situations and later math studies.

Even with all the practice situations in hands-on math, there are still situations where facts just have to be memorized. The key to good teaching is to know who needs the practice and when. At Halifax Independent School, work from textbooks provides this practice, and there are many creative ways of drilling facts, including computer programs. This drill and practice will continue throughout middle school, as forgetting is human, but drills are used judiciously and tailored to the needs of individuals.

INDIVIDUAL DIFFERENCES AND LEARNING STYLES

There is huge variation in the ease and speed at which children absorb new math concepts. Some children seem to instinctively "know" that 6 x 8 is 48, whereas others find it painful to learn and remember. I know a child who, by the age of three, already knew that 4 + 6 was 10 and could figure out any simple addition in his head (he now has a PhD in theoretical physics). However, most children at that age are still struggling with one-to-one correspondence and learning the skill of counting (accurately) up to five.

In the middle elementary years, teachers observe when children move from using manipulatives to solve problems to figuring things out in their heads — moving from the concrete to the symbolic level. The variation is huge, for example, in how long children will need to use counters to figure out 5 + 3. Of course, we'd like them to be able to "just know" the answer and eventually they will, but that usually takes time, and knowing how to find the answer and when to apply it is more important. Schools have to fill the needs both of the few five-year-olds who are easily counting to one thousand and the many who struggle to count out five objects. Does it make sense to teach all of them the same way? What accounts for these individual differences, and is there a way to reach all of them?

Fascinating new research at Duke University by Park and Brannen[45] posits the existence of an approximate number system (ANS) or intuitive sense of number. This pre-verbal ability allows us to estimate approximate numbers in the absence of symbols, and recent research has shown that there is a correlation between "the acuity of the ANS and performance in symbolic math throughout development and into adulthood, which suggests that the ANS may serve as a cognitive foundation for the uniquely human capacity for symbolic math." Six-month-old babies show a large variation in the ability to recognize changes in numbers of dots, a pre-verbal number ability that correlates with their math scores as three-and-a-half-year-olds. The researchers concluded, "mathematics is built upon an intuitive sense of number that predates language."[46]

Developing this innate number sense, or ANS, is crucial for mathematics education, and lots of practice with manipulatives and hands-on, real-life activities are absolutely essential for helping children with a weaker ANS to strengthen it and develop their understanding of number. But this type of learning also works well with children with more developed ANS, since its open-ended nature allows for "discoveries" beyond those that were predicted.

> One of the first mathematical concepts that children learn is the concept of number — what does seven mean? How is it different from five? Another fundamental concept is the idea of equivalence: two sets of objects can be equivalent even if they are arranged differently. Thus, when children start school, they spend lots of time learning to count, and putting objects into groups.
>
> This class of five-year-olds is learning about writing equations and about some of the ways the number five can be represented. They are using Cuisenaire rods, brightly coloured blocks that are fun to play with, and with which they have had ample opportunity to play freely.
>
> The teacher hands out stapled booklets to the five children in the group, and they go to the table with the Cuisenaire rods. The children open their booklets at the page they have been working on, which looks like this:

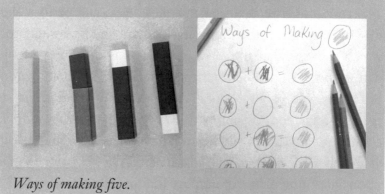

Ways of making five.

> The coloured rods are based on the white centimetre cube, which represents one, or one tenth, or, in the case of these young children, just itself. The next largest is the red one, which is two centimetres long. The light green is three centimetres, and so on up to the ten-centimetre orange one. The children have been playing with them for some time, and can make staircases and other patterns with them.
>
> When they find their place at the table, the children find a yellow rod and two rods that equal it, colouring in the sheet for each combination. Some of them notice that light green plus red equals yellow, as does red plus light green. When they think they have all the combinations they move on to the next page. Lots of chatting is happening as the children compare their results or point out a discovery.

The casual observer of these five-year-olds might conclude that they were all just playing. However, serious exploration and practice of skills is occurring while they are having fun. This group was practising writing equations (even if they are pre-numeric) while at the same time learning about fundamental relationships between numbers. These five-year-olds exploring with the Cuisenaire rods are learning about the "fiveness of five" by comparing it with other rods. They will observe that the yellow (five) rod is bigger than the pink one, but smaller than the brown. They learn that light green plus red makes yellow. They might notice that two yellow rods together make one orange rod. Soon they will be attaching numbers to the colours. In other math activities, they will learn about counting out five objects, what five on a die looks like, and that they have five digits on each hand. Children who have a solid sense of "what is five?" will move quickly through these activities, often making many interesting discoveries of their own on the way.

Children have different abilities within the different branches of mathematics. For instance, one child might have difficulty with adding, subtracting and remembering number facts, but at the same time have excellent spatial awareness and be very good at fitting pattern pieces together. I have often taught children who had excellent recall of the multiplication tables, but who froze when asked to solve a problem where they had to decide which operation to use. The skill in teaching math is to know the children and their abilities and to take these differences into account. The problem with traditional math is that it treats all children the same, and the discouragement felt by a child who doesn't do well memorizing math facts can turn them off other branches of math in which they could actually excel.

There are many ways to address students' individual needs, and one of the most exciting is the growing use of computers in the classroom. There are many math websites available that can challenge those who are ready for it with interesting problems, motivate others with fun games and activities and help everyone with solidifying the basic facts through math video games. A word of caution, though: many computer math activities are merely computerized versions of playing with math manipulatives. For young children, the tactile experience of putting blocks together or arranging tangram pieces is important for their development; manipulating them in two dimensions on a computer does not have the same effect.

MOTIVATION

Motivation in mathematics is essential — an inconvenient fact that is often overlooked by those arguing for a return to traditional teaching. I would argue that the widespread math fears that exist in the world mean that making the subject enjoyable is more critical for mathematics than for learning in other areas. I cannot tell you how many times parents have told me that "they were no good in math" and expressed surprise that their children were actually doing well. Or, conversely, if their children were experiencing difficulties, they might say, "Oh, it must be genetic." These attitudes can be passed on to their children by osmosis. The media and business don't help, with gender stereotyping and general assumptions that being good at math is just not cool.

Traditional math teaching, with its emphasis on testing and mastery of basic skills by rote, is largely responsible for this math fear/phobia. Discouragement, failure and boredom resulting from mindless memorizing of seemingly meaningless facts or pages of calculations can quickly make almost any student "hate" math. Once children feel they can't do math and/or they "hate" the subject, it is very difficult for them to be open to new concepts. I have worked with many children (and adults) who decided in elementary school that math was not their thing, often because they had failed tests or had had long traumatic experiences of not understanding concepts and then trying to remember methods that didn't make sense to them. And once they got the message that they didn't have a "math brain," they clearly decided there was no point in really trying.

Tests, marks and rankings, the extrinsic motivators that are shown in other chapters of this book to be the least effective methods of getting children to work, can actually contribute to de-motivation, especially in math. At Halifax Independent and many schools where hands-on math is taught, "playing" with manipulatives to solve problems and doing interesting activities that allow them to investigate mathematical concepts keeps children engaged. Games, cooperative group problem solving and whole-group mental math activities help reinforce some of the basic facts, while individual practice (working from texts or work sheets) is put in the context of mastering operations. When children see mathematics as something that can be enjoyable or even beautiful, and when they are confident in their own ability, they are more motivated to persist at it, even when it becomes challenging.

Anyone who doubts that hands-on math and manipulatives are intrinsically motivating for children should visit Halifax Independent School on a rainy day when there is "indoor snack" and time for free play. The math manipulatives are some of the most popular things to play with — you will see children building structures with Cuisenaire rods, elaborate patterns with pattern blocks or towns with Base 10 blocks.

Hands-on math teachers appreciate the importance of knowing each child so they can keep everyone motivated, thus avoiding the boredom and possible failure that plague traditional math classes. They know when children need extra support (often simply more "hands-on" time working at the concrete level) and when they need a challenge. The open-ended nature of the activities allows both.

> Hands-on math does not prescribe how math is taught, but generally classes at Halifax Independent School start with a whole-class activity to generate interest and present a new concept. This is followed by small group activities where children may work on different aspects of the new concept. Generally everyone gets a chance to do all the activities over the course of a few days, but this is a place where teachers can tailor activities to different ability levels.
>
> For example, a class of ten- and eleven-year-olds learning about two-digit multiplication starts off with a quick game of "I have . . . who has . . .?" Each child has a small card with a multiplication question

on one side and a different answer on the other. One child starts off by standing up and asking the question on their card: "Who has 8 x 4?" Another child jumps up, saying, "I have 32, who has 9 x 3?" and so on, until everyone has had a turn and the first child answers, "I have . . ." (whatever number was on their card). The class can challenge itself to finish the round faster than the previous day.

After this particular class collectively groans because they took eight seconds longer to finish the game than the day before, the teacher settles them down at their tables and, using an overhead projector, illustrates multiplying two-digit numbers by using examples on a grid.

She models 28 x 13 by showing 13 rows of 28 squares, groups them into blocks of 20 x 10, 10 x 8, 20 x 3 and 8 x 3. Together, they add up all numbers and come up with a total. A brief discussion ensues, and then the teacher hands out grid paper and asks them all to figure out another problem using the same method. After a few more questions, the children put the sheets in their math binders, and get ready to find out their group assignments for the day.

One group must find the area of rectangles using the two-digit multiplication they have just learned (from last week's lesson on area). The last few questions ask them to measure several objects in the classroom and find the area. Another group works on a page of two-digit multiplication from a textbook. A group is working on the floor with Base 10 blocks, gathering 12 groups of 32, sorting them into rods and units and figuring out the total number. The final group of four children is poring over a problem involving measuring carpets for a house, and figuring out the various costs — these children have shown that they understand multi-digit multiplication and have mastered their multiplication tables.

After about half an hour, the groups change. Unfinished work goes into their binders, awaiting "finish up" day on Friday. The problem-solving group continues to work on their problem.

Making trains with Cuisenaire rods.

This case study has four more advanced students working on a problem of measuring carpets for a house; they are applying the multiplication and geometry skills they have mastered, while also solving problems and working collaboratively. They are extending their learning and seeing real-life applications for multiplication. They are being challenged, and for these students, that is what keeps them motivated. At other times, they could be exploring fascinating relationships found in Pascal's triangle or the Fibonacci theorem or solving logic problems — all glimpses into the deeper mysteries of math. The really wonderful thing about this type of teaching is what happens when the children share what they are doing with others in the class — the excitement that they feel is contagious and can often motivate others.

MATH TEACHING IN THE NEWS

Educational change in the public system takes time, especially when it is about the teaching of math. Many parents — and, truth be told, teachers — feel intimidated when confronted with math teaching methodologies that are new to them. Since so many of us struggled with math at school ourselves, sometimes just looking at a child's homework that involves a method we aren't familiar with is enough to bring back all those anxieties. Even those of us who are confident in math, or who use it in our jobs, can become frustrated when trying to help our children if they insist on using a different method than we know.

Once again, there have been calls to go back to the old ways. The day after the 2012 PISA results were released in December 2013, John Manley, CEO of the Canadian Council of Chief Executives, declared in a *Globe and Mail* article, "This is on the scale of a national emergency," all because Canada had slipped from the top ten in the rankings in its math scores among fifteen-year-olds. He went on to make some dire predictions about Canada's future in the global economy because of our falling math scores. The same article described Canada's "poor international math performance" and stated, "Canada did not fare too well in reading or science either." It then predictably went on to quote an academic's call for a "reform movement to restore some of the basics into math education."[47]

This was only the day after the release of the results, and no one in Canada, not least the reporter, had had a chance to examine them in detail. But even a quick look at the results indicate that, although Canada had indeed slipped from sixth to thirteenth in the rankings, part of the drop could be explained by the addition of several new countries. More important would be to look at the annual average score — Canada's was 518 out of a total of 700, a slippage over twelve years of testing of about 2 per cent. Of concern, perhaps, but not exactly a national emergency! Canada still outperformed all the other English speaking countries (the US's average score was 481, the UK's 494) and was well over the OECD average of 490.[48]

Canada's more hands-on approach to math than many other countries can perhaps take credit for its relatively high levels of "equity" as measured on the PISA tests: "The PISA results of several countries demonstrate that high average performance and equity are not mutually exclusive. Australia, Canada, Estonia, Finland, Hong Kong-China, Japan, Korea, Liechtenstein and Macao-China show above-OECD-average mean performance and a weak relationship between socio-economic status and student performance."[49]

Nevertheless, the press immediately jumped on the "new math" or "discovery math" as it was dubbed. I think what they mean by discovery math is what I have described in this chapter, and call "hands-on" math, but it is not a term used by many teachers. To read some of the articles, one is left with the impression that in a "discovery" math classroom, children are allowed to play with a bunch of math materials in a completely unstructured way and left to discover all the mathematical relationships by themselves. Since then, there have been petitions from parents demanding changes, and studies commissioned.

Rebellion in Alberta

Let's look at the province whose math scores on PISA have declined the most dramatically over the nine years that the tests have been carried out: Alberta, whose score declined thirty-six points in all. There could be many reasons for this decline, and although pointing the finger at the "new way" of teaching math is easy scapegoating, it is not borne out by the facts. For one thing, over half the drop in scores (nineteen points) occurred between 2003 and 2006, well before the math curriculum was overhauled in 2007. During that decade, Alberta was the fastest growing province in Canada, with its population increasing by over one third between 2001 and 2012, and immigrants to Canada comprising about one fifth of these newcomers. One possible explanation of the declining scores is the strain on the school system caused by this increasing population, especially with an influx of non-English-speaking students.

But the Alberta math curriculum became a scapegoat for the back-to-basics movement. An organization called WISE Math (Western Initiative for Strengthening Education in Math) was formed, petitions were signed and conferences held, all damning "discovery math." The culmination of this movement was the publication of a CD Howe report in 2015 entitled, "What to Do about Canada's Declining Math Scores." It was subtitled "With mounting evidence showing the short-comings of discovery-based instruction, it's time to put more emphasis on direct instruction."[50] The report, written by Anna Stokke, a math professor at University of Manitoba, is full of references to "convoluted" methods that strain a child's working memory and make her feel stupid, and cites research that apparently proves it. However, Ann Kajander, a math education professor and author of several books promoting creativity in math teaching, says of the report, "How can we have a report that makes significant recommendations in mathematics education when absolutely none of the major mathematics education journals . . . are included in the reference list? As a researcher, that's absurd."[51]

> After receiving a petition with seventeen thousand signatures calling for a return to teaching standard algorithms and reducing time spent on patterns and manipulatives, as well as ditching the inquiry method in all subjects, the Department of Education issued a "Bulletin for Teachers":[52] "Some parents may have heard the term 'discovery math' used to describe the mathematics program. This term does not accurately describe the program."
>
> Instead of backtracking on the methodology and succumbing to demands to teach by rote and drill basic skills, the department chose to clarify that memorizing and understanding number facts are both part of "mastery," that teachers are free to teach different strategies and children can use whatever works for them, but that they need to understand why it works: " . . . if the child does not understand why the strategy works, she or he will not be able to build on the concept for future learning."

WHAT DO WE WANT CHILDREN TO GET FROM THEIR MATH EDUCATION?

Some business leaders and governments worry that Canada won't be able to compete in the global economy, falling behind Asian economies, because we can't produce more top-rate mathematicians to lead the way. Perhaps this is true, but what is the best way to produce them? Is it traditional math teaching, with its emphasis on direct instruction, basic skills and memorization? The back-to-basics crowd ignores the fact that with traditional math, many children with great potential will just fall by the wayside.

The goal of hands-on math is to give every child a positive attitude, a good basic grounding (enough to enable them to pursue math education as far as they want) and the critical thinking/problem solving skills they will need. Most provincial departments of education now fortunately reflect this.

Hands-on math, particularly in the elementary and middle school years, will produce more high school students ready to take on the challenge of advanced math. We will also graduate citizens who are not afraid of math, and who will be motivated to pursue math education as far as they need to. They will be better critical thinkers than the apocryphal superintendent of education who insisted he didn't care what the teachers did as long as all their students scored above average on the standardized test (a mathematical impossibility).[53]

Traditional math teaching favours those students who grasp concepts quickly and also have a high tolerance for the subsequent boredom as everyone else in the class catches up. Successful students have to get lots of satisfaction out of completing pages of drill questions quickly, score highly on the tests, have no problem memorizing their multiplication tables and know on their own when to apply a particular operation to solve a problem. Traditional mathematics teaching has clear rules, but it can also be dry and boring, and it turns off many promising students who may later discover their math talents. Although I did honours math in university, I nearly missed promotion to Grade 4 because I didn't know my math facts. If I had been held back early on, I could have been turned off math completely.

For those many students who struggle under traditional math teaching, math class is often a mystifying experience as they try, like Anne, to apply seemingly random algorithms to meaningless questions. Who doesn't remember learning the procedure for long division? It's hard enough for everyone, but for those who don't understand why or when we need to divide, it is a recipe for frustration and discouragement.

Traditional math in the elementary and middle school years was largely based on arithmetic, and calculation was a huge part of it. As time goes on, many more "strands" of mathematics have been added to the curriculum, at earlier ages. At Halifax Independent, I was teaching children math concepts that I didn't learn myself until late high school and university: transformational geometry, logic, algebra and statistics to name a few. Presenting them early to children in a hands-on way gives all of them an understanding of the underlying concepts that will help them later on.

For example, I would introduce algebra to children as young as eight or nine by letting them experience balancing two sides of an equation with an actual scale and weighted numbers. Putting a weighted 7 on one side, and a 5 on the other, it would be the child's job to find the number that would make the scale balance. The equation would be written $7 = 5 + \_\_\_\_\_$. After lots of experience with equations like this (and different ways of weighing numbers and counters), it is a short step to substituting an x for the _____ so that the equation reads $7 = 5 + x$, $x = _____$. When children are comfortable with this concept, they are less likely to express what a new middle school student I was helping once said to me, "I thought math was supposed to be about numbers. What are all these letters doing here?"

Coding and basic programming are being introduced in many elementary schools now, giving children some basic tools that will allow them to take their interest in computers to the next level. By being exposed to so many different branches of mathematics, children will often find an area that resonates with them, and experiencing success in one branch will increase their confidence overall.

I believe most parents want their children to enjoy math and to have a good enough grounding in the basic concepts to decide whether or not they wish to pursue higher math. Hands-on math in the elementary years will give all children, even those who later choose not to go on with math, the positive outlook, deeper understanding and problem-solving skills that will benefit them in whatever career they choose.

SMALL CLASSES

Teaching hands-on math is highly dependent on knowing each child's learning style, stage of development and preferences. Groups need to be flexible and constantly changing. Some children may have difficulty with operations and number sense, but easily master spatial awareness or pattern recognition. Small classes allow the teacher to observe each child, recognizing when they need more reinforcement of a concept (or more time to work at a concrete level) and when they are ready to move on. It allows more time for individual explanations, which are often just what is needed to provide that "Eureka!" moment for a child who may have struggled to understand whole-group instruction, or who for some reason has missed the introduction of a concept. One of the most rewarding moments in math teaching happens when, after observing a child work through a problem that has been troubling her, the teacher is able to pinpoint exactly what is causing her confusion and provide an explanation that makes sense. The lighting up of a child's face as she solves yet another mystery of math, getting closer to the deep beauty that is mathematics, is a moment of shared joy between teacher and student.

Planning and execution for this type of mathematics teaching can be more time consuming and complex than for a traditional classroom. In a "vertical" (teacher-led) classroom, the teacher usually stands at the front of the class to explain concepts, often using the blackboard (or, today, perhaps a SMART Board) to illustrate the ideas. The primary relationship is between the teacher and the students. In a traditional math class, planning the lesson may consist of preparing a short presentation or demonstration, assigning pages in a text, finding worksheets or drills to reinforce the concept, and of course, marking the results.

In a progressive classroom, using a "horizontal" teaching style where the teacher is a facilitator, the students work cooperatively together, and the central relationship is among the students. A "horizontal" teaching style using hands-on methods requires all of the above planning, plus monitoring the groups, finding stimulating and appropriate investigations and observing students. Planning becomes more complex the more students there are in the class. Hands-on learning often takes more time to teach as it is important that each child gets to experience the joy of discovering new concepts for himself. The larger the classes are, the more difficult it is to ensure that each child gets these opportunities.

INTEGRATION OF MATH INTO OTHER CURRICULUM AREAS

Even though math is taught as a separate subject at Halifax Independent, math teachers work closely with others to find opportunities to integrate math skills into other areas. Theme teaching and inquiry-based classrooms integrate mathematics into the curriculum in many ways. For instance, various themes in which building occurs (building a playhouse or playground structure) require multiple mathematical skills: measurement (finding the lengths of building materials and angles needed), multiplication (how much will it cost for 23 board feet at 16 cents a board foot?), division (how many 1.5 foot lengths can be cut from an 8-foot 2 x 4?) and area (how many 2 x 3-foot pieces can be cut from one piece of plywood?) are all used.

If a class is studying space, by comparing the relative diameters of the planets or estimating distances between Earth and various stars (trying to find out which are closest), they are reinforcing working with large numbers and scientific notation. During the World of Work theme one year, my ten- and eleven-year-olds did a survey on work-life balance among family members. The data collected became the basis for much graphing and statistical analysis in math class, and the report that was produced became part of the Fair presentation — parents were quite interested in how they compared to the average!

The more math can be integrated into other learning situations, and the more it can be rooted in practical, real-life situations, the more the students see its relevance to their lives. The connections children make ensure that they are constantly reminded of the utility of learning math and its importance. When they see that math has a purpose in the real world and is not just an abstraction, they are more motivated to work at it. As with language skills, the more they use their math abilities in other situations, the more proficient they will be.

HANDS-ON MATH LEADS TO GREATER UNDERSTANDING — FOR EVERYONE

Math teaching has gone through several incarnations in the last forty years. The latest version of hands-on math has stumbled in the public school system along the way. When a new program is introduced, there is always a period of transition in which all teachers may not get adequate training in the new methods. This can lead to feelings of uncertainty or to some teachers lapsing back into "tried and true" old-school methods. Parents can be bewildered when confronted with homework that looks nothing like what they would have received in school. Increased training for teachers, better resources and better communication with parents should go a long way to improving math teaching, without compromising the program.

Even non-teachers who are very confident in their math abilities can benefit from seeing how young children actually learn mathematical concepts. At Halifax Independent, open math classes where parents are invited to come to class and participate in the various activities with their children help them understand the different strategies they are learning.

From time to time, Halifax Independent holds a whole-school math fair or math fun night for parents and children to demystify what goes on in the classroom. Math manipulatives and math games and activities that parents can try with their children are set up in each classroom. Displays of children's work adorn the walls, and the children take the lead, showing off their work and helping the parents navigate their way through the problems. They can wander through the classrooms and see how math is taught at the different levels.

Newsletters about what is going on in math help explain the how and why of the strategies that the children may use. Parents also help by giving feedback to the teachers about how their children are doing with math activities at home. The teachers appreciate knowing if a child has really struggled at home with a particular concept. When parents understand how their children are being taught, they can initiate conversations with their children about the strategies they use to calculate or solve problems and show them that they are impressed. Having a child teach a parent a new way of doing something helps them develop their math vocabulary, express themselves mathematically and may open the parent's eyes to a new world of math.

When children at Halifax Independent struggle with some aspects of math, the teachers' recommendations for parents who want to help at home does not generally include math workbooks or math tutoring agencies. These can sometimes exacerbate whatever problems the child is having and cause resentment. They are more likely to recommend math games, computer activities, books of fun math problems and building things together. The important thing is that the activities are enjoyable for both parent or caregiver and child.

Hands-on math has been practised at Halifax Independent School for over forty years, and it is responsible for more children enjoying math and feeling successful at it than at any other school I have taught. There has not been a scientific follow-up study, but anecdotal reports from graduates and their parents tell me that there have been many graduates who have excelled in high school math, winning math contests and going on to do sciences at university.

But that is not the whole story. Just as significant are the many average math students who have done well in high school math, and often gone on to use math in their careers. And most rewarding of all are the weaker students who, in spite of their challenges, have maintained a positive attitude and approach mathematical issues with an open mind. This has been possible because of Halifax Independent's focus on giving all children hands-on experiences to entrench basic mathematical concepts and skills, thus gently encouraging them to love math.

Chapter 4
NOT JUST FRILLS — ARTS EDUCATION

"The arts especially address the idea of aesthetic experience. An aesthetic experience is one in which your senses are operating at their peak; when you're present in the current moment; when you're resonating with the excitement of this thing that you're experiencing; when you are fully alive."
— Sir Ken Robinson

"An educational system isn't worth a great deal if it teaches young people how to make a living but doesn't teach them how to make a life."
— Unknown

Our children's education has to be about much more than just preparing them for the job market; it should be about cultivating multi-dimensional human beings who, as well as being good citizens, will have the capacity to appreciate the magnificence of this world we live in. Education in visual arts, music, drama and dance encourages imagination and creativity, and allows children to discover capabilities that they might not otherwise know they have. It provides times of true cooperation and sharing, when children really feel what it means to be part of a team or community.

Education in the arts also improves scholastic achievement. Legions of studies over the years have shown how music participation in school leads to higher academic achievement,[54] and higher SAT scores.[55] Music training has even been shown to increase the cortical thickness in the brain, leading to beneficial effects on attention span, anxiety management and emotional control, all of which are highly correlated with academic achievement but are important for success in life as well.[56]

Although music has been studied most widely, similar results have been found with other arts subjects. But all these studies, while worthwhile, are missing the main point: the arts are intrinsically valuable in themselves. Many adults spend their leisure time appreciating, if not creating, some form of art, and arts production is a huge sector of society on its own.

Arts education also gives children the opportunity to feel complete absorption in creating something, when they are so completely absorbed in an activity that they lose track of time and experience a feeling of happiness or even ecstasy. The ability to experience this sense of "flow" has been associated with increased life satisfaction derived from personal development and growth.

When I was in high school I learned to play the euphonium. Some of my happiest memories are of playing in the band, and although I never considered myself particularly talented or musical, I missed playing after I graduated. After many years I took it up again and finally joined the local sixty-piece concert band, which played at a level way above mine. At first I struggled to keep up, and I was in constant anxiety during concerts. However, as I practised and got better, concerts became more enjoyable. In recent

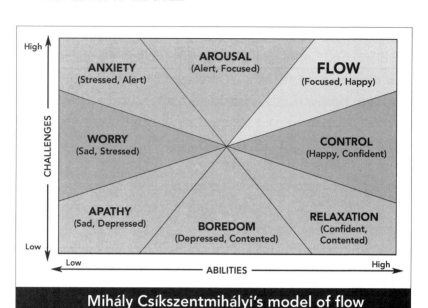

Flow diagram — challenge level vs skill level.

years, there have even been times during concerts when the band was playing well, and so was I, that I experienced what I think is "flow" — this feeling of intense concentration, with occasional flashes of joy. This never would have happened had I not had the base level of skill that came from my school musical education.

My band experience illustrates that flow is more likely to happen when the skill level and the challenge of the activity is high. This is the purpose of arts education in the public schools; it is not to create legions of professional musicians or artists, but to give all children some skills and expose them to an appreciation for a wide variety of arts practices. As children get older, providing they have this base, they can choose to deepen their experience with particular areas of the arts — either within school or even thirty years later!

Chalmers Doane and Halifax All-City Music

In the late 1960s, a far-sighted superintendent of music, Chalmers Doane, convinced the Halifax School Board to spend new money on an enhanced music program for city schools. By 1979, twenty-one new full-time music specialists were hired, a music resource centre set up and instruments bought to outfit bands and orchestras. Starting in elementary school, every child had music at least twice a week, taught with the Kodaly method, which emphasized listening, movement, rhythm and singing in the early stages. Students learned voice to begin with, ukulele and recorder from Grade 3 and by Grade 5 they could choose between strings or band. At that point they could benefit from before- and after-school classes on their particular instrument with specialists, and after a few years could take part in various ensembles around the city. An auditioned ukulele group gained a very high profile, as did the Symphony Orchestra, an All City Band and various choirs. Enrolment was enormous, and consisted of children from all areas of the city and all socio-economic levels.

The success of Doane's music program was the result of many factors — a progressive climate that valued the arts, a growing economy and a booming population. But mostly it was Doane's vision, his ability to persuade administrators to spend money and his personal contribution to the formation of the musical groups that contributed to the success of the program.

One of those early choir teachers told me that when she worked with children from kindergarten on, over 95 per cent of the students could be taught to sing in tune.[57] How many of us who didn't benefit from a program like that can actually sing in tune?

In those days, it was a common sight to see quite young children lugging cellos and trombones off to school. As a result, the generations that benefited from Chalmers Doane's music program have contributed to the lively music scene in Halifax today — there

> are more live music venues in Halifax per capita than any other city in Canada, and many well-known bands and musical groups got their start here. But most telling is the number of amateur bands, orchestras, choirs and other musical ensembles that enliven the city cultural scene. And although the music program in the schools has diminished somewhat since those days, it is still a vibrant part of school life for many children.

INTEGRATING ARTS INTO THE CURRICULUM

One of the fundamental principles of the theme studies approach is that skills and subject matter are presented in a hands-on, integrated way. The given topic is investigated deeply through many different spheres — the more ways children experience the same principle, the more opportunities they have for practising the related skills and the more they will understand. Integrating music, art, drama and dance deepens the learning and reaches children on a different level. At Halifax Independent School, the arts are both mixed into the regular program and taught in classes with specialist art, music and drama teachers.

One of the reasons for having, for example, a full-time music teacher is to give them a lot of opportunity to organize musical activities that complement what the regular classes are doing in theme, in addition to teaching their own curriculum. When the five-year-olds were studying the senses in theme, they made simple instruments in music class and looked at how sound is transmitted through the air to the ear. And when the theme was the World of Work, the Grade 5/6 class studied labour issues in the early twentieth century in their regular class. In music class they learned old work songs as well as early union songs — a musical and poetical representation of the issues that deepened the learning.

Drumming group at the spring music concert.

The yearly theme is Discovery, and Maggie, who teaches music to the youngest children in the school, has talked to them about the connection between music and math. All of her music classes for the first half of the school year will focus on exploring patterns and numbers in music. It will culminate in the concert in February, where the children will guide the audience through this discovery process, showing them musical versions of mathematical patterns and illustrations of the mathematics of music.

The six- and seven-year-olds troop into the classroom singing, "B, A, G, B, A, G . . ." to the tune of "Hot Cross Buns." They take their seats in pairs facing each other, and Maggie reminds them of the geometric transformations they have been working on in math — slides, rotations and flips. "Today, we are going to look at flips, at mirror images, and you are all going to get a chance to be mirrors." She starts playing the piano, and on a cue, one child in the pair does an action, while the other child mirrors it. It takes some

> time and discussion before they all get the idea, but soon they are all participating enthusiastically.
>
> Then, a projection of the music for Hot Cross Buns appears on the wall with the notes labelled, and underneath is a mirror image of the tune, in which the notes go up instead of down, "B, C, D, B, C, D . . ." The children take out their recorders and learn some new notes (C and D), and they begin playing the familiar tune. After a few minutes, they play the "mirror" version, and before long the class is playing both versions at the same time — a surprisingly harmonious sound from such young children!
>
> Finally, the class ends with everyone being conductors, and learning to count one, two, three, four, with number one as the downbeat. The children practise making a square with their hands, and then conduct to the sound of Mozart's "Eine Kleine Nachtmusik." Maggie tells them about how some people think that the patterns in Mozart's music help "organize our brains." The children watch a "synesthesia" version of the music, where instead of notes, the music is displayed as a series of rectangles that flash by in time to the music. The patterns are easy to see, and the children are busy trying to figure out how it works as they conduct enthusiastically. They are still talking about it as they leave the classroom.

Exploring a topic through art deepens children's understanding of the topic while giving them new skills. Some children who may have difficulties expressing themselves in words or writing find that they can excel in artistic expression; children with difficulty reading may be able to delve more deeply into a topic using pictures. When the Grade 5/6 class studied labour issues, for example, they decided (prompted by the art teacher) to explore the genre of street or graffiti art. They looked at examples of protest and graffiti art, and then, using tracings of their own bodies, created a mural that

Mural painting — giving it everything you've got!

encapsulated the various issues being studied. Each child came up with a slogan for their particular issue (child labour, workplace safety or working conditions). Having to distill all that they had learned into a protest slogan required them to analyze, synthesize and evaluate, all of which are higher order skills. The mural was the highlight of their Fair presentation and was an excellent example of how collaboration and integration between teachers of different disciplines can enhance and enrich both classes.

Although the arts are fully integrated into the regular Halifax Independent School curriculum, the children still need specialist teachers who can pass on ways of seeing, techniques of expression and skill development methodologies that the regular classroom teacher just does not know. The most successful arts programs offer this specialist-integration quality; where this happens, regular classroom teachers

Elders' mural — street art and workplace issues.

usually also need more professional development, especially in "sustained, hands-on art-making," if only to keep up with the level of artistic expression of their students. As a recent report on arts education states, "Once teachers see themselves as artists . . . the transition to bring arts into the classroom becomes more fluid."[58]

Musical theatre is an ideal way to integrate the arts into every elementary school year. Putting on a play or musical allows students to experience singing, dancing and acting, as well as making sets and props, all while producing something important. The variety of tasks available means that everyone can find a niche and feel the satisfaction of contributing to a big event. On the surface, it is easy to see how children's artistic and musical skills are enhanced by participating in musical theatre. On a deeper level, however, children are also learning hugely valuable social skills. Cooperation, working to deadlines and delivering on

Rehearsing for the Plays.

time are enormously important workplace skills — there is no deadline quite as firm as when the curtain goes up on opening night! Although musical theatre is often seen as an extra-curricular activity, at Halifax Independent School it is incorporated into the curriculum.

THE PLAYS

Every year, the whole elementary school abandons the regular schedule for approximately two weeks, and goes into production mode for four plays. The children are heavily invested in the process, as the plays are written by the four older elementary classes. Every child has a role to play. The children make all the props and scenery, and they make their own costumes at home. In the end, the final production is a quirky, amusing showcase of the children's originality and artistic talents, but the point of it all is the skills they learn along the way.

Making props often starts with papier mâché.

Two weeks of play-acting? Aren't the children going to fall behind in their academics? This section will show that although Play time can be considered an in-depth literacy unit, much more is happening. It is a time when teachers use all their skills to draw out the creativity of individual children, helping them blend their ideas into those of the group so they experience working as a cohesive whole. The children get a great deal of pride and satisfaction from working cooperatively, with deadlines, to produce something that will delight and entertain.

Play production
The first day of Play production is highly anticipated, as it is the day the children find out which of the four plays they will be in, as well as their role. It starts out with a meeting, as does each day, and each morning of the two weeks is divided into four forty-five-minute periods consisting of rehearsal,

A Dalhousie Co-operative School play — Pirates and Pickled Herring.

props, math activity and literacy activity. The children are divided into four multi-class groups for these activities, and again put in pairs of older and younger students, and they rotate through the four activities.

The first rehearsal begins with a reading of the whole script, with everyone taking their roles, and the older students helping their younger partners with the reading. Highlighters are used for children to mark their scripts, and they are sent off to help each other learn their lines. By the third or fourth day, blocking is added, as the classroom becomes a make-believe stage and children learn about movement, gestures and expression. As props are finished, they are delivered to the rehearsal rooms, and add a new dimension for the children, who no longer have to mime using them. During the second week, more intensive small group practice occurs, while still running through the entire play to ensure continuity. Once lines are learned, it is possible to workshop the plays a little, drawing out the humour or emphasizing the suspense. The last few days are spent rehearsing on the real stage rented from a local theatre — a vital step, as this transition can be very exciting or traumatic for some children. The directors work with the stage crew on lighting, sound and curtain calls, and everyone becomes familiar and comfortable with the backstage areas as well as the stage itself.

The props classroom, where each group comes to create the props and backdrops for the four plays, quickly begins to look like an artist's workshop. Drying racks hold painted leaves or vines, tubs of white goop are waiting to have piles of ripped up newspaper soaked in them, and stands of cardboard bushes are being constructed. Large sheets of mural paper are in the process of being painted to represent kitchen scenes, a castle on a hill or the inside of a spaceship. Piles of shredded yellow paper await gluing to a roof to represent thatch. As the weeks progress, the racks fill up with the finished props. The larger-than-life papier-mâché cups, jugs, cell phones and hairbrushes give the room the aura of a giant's kitchen.

The other two activities in which the children participate every day are designed to counteract the excitement that tends to build up in rehearsals and props. They are generally quieter, and more academically oriented activities, such as math-based art in which the children delve into concepts like tessellations, patterns, fractals and snowflake designs.

Every afternoon begins in the lunchroom, with a whole-school rehearsal of the finale song. This song, set to a familiar-to-the-parents tune, always has a rousing chorus and one verse that describes each of the four plays. The rest of the afternoons are generally spent in the children's own

Art math — rotation patterns.

classrooms doing finish-up work and other projects that involve mostly independent work. However, the directors use this time to work with some small groups who need more practice, and to rehearse a final dance with each play.

The big night finally arrives, and excited children are delivered backstage at the theatre. Extra staff and volunteers are on hand to help the children don their costumes, keep them calm and amused in their dressing rooms, and deliver them to the stage at the right time. The directors are giving instructions to the stage technicians, acting as prompters and ensuring that all the props are in the right places. The middle-school students are present, many dressed in black, moving props backstage, playing in the pit band or doing sound effects. In between plays, they have prepared various physical theatre "entr'actes," which they perform in front of the curtains. When the last dance has finished, all the children and adults involved assemble on stage for the finale song, and are then collected by their parents. On the way out, each child collects a cherished prop from their play, which they have chosen earlier as a souvenir. The children happily accept their accolades, while their parents wonder what on earth they will do with the six-foot cardboard pirate ship they have suddenly acquired.

What is being learned?
One way of looking at the Plays is as an in-depth literacy unit in which the children write the plays, and then go through the whole process of rehearsing and staging them. Being involved in every aspect of the process makes it a truly authentic writing experience. The children experience writing for a purpose, rewriting, workshopping, reading, memorizing and presenting to an audience. They are working on their communication skills every minute of the unit.

Another way to look at the Plays is that this period is an immersion in the arts. From beginning to the end, the children are participating in creating props, painting scenery, designing costumes, learning songs and performing dances. They are intensely involved in learning such dramatic arts as portraying emotion, projection and movement. They learn about what goes on behind the scenes to stage theatrical productions. In short, it accomplishes all the goals of an arts education outlined in this chapter.

The cooperation involved in putting on the plays, and the collaboration needed for their writing teach important social lessons. The children will remember the sense of togetherness they felt while singing the finale song. Surmounting the general sag in spirits when rehearsals aren't going well, helping a younger child remember their lines or overcoming stage fright are all experiences that children will remember and draw on as they grow up.

But my favourite moments in the Plays are those when the classroom or stage becomes the undersea Gully or interior of a Rajah's palace, and the children are no longer acting, but actually experiencing their make-believe world come alive. Then you know that the magic of the theatre has made an impression on them.

THE PENDULUM SWINGS

Progressive educational ideas were prominent during the period between the two world wars, and then again in the late 1960s and early 1970s. Arts education flourished in these periods. But more recently, the pendulum has swung in the other direction, and arts education is often referred to as a "frill." As in the US and Britain, a combination of cutbacks in funding and emphasis on test scores in the core subjects has sharply reduced the number and quality of arts programs, and limited access to them in Canadian schools.[59]

The best arts programs in public schools are generally in affluent urban neighbourhoods, where parents can also afford private lessons. Poor children are doubly disadvantaged if they don't attend arts-rich schools; their parents can't afford private programs, and a growing number of students graduate having never been exposed to good arts teaching.

Arts education is not a frill, and it does have an impact on all areas of education — as we have seen. We live in a society that has moved beyond the basics, and if we want our children to have the creativity and insight they will need to contribute in this century, we need to ensure they all have a good experience with the arts.

WANT TO DIRECT A PLAY, ANYONE?

Where good arts programs exist in schools, it is often because of the efforts of the parents. Sometimes this is through school councils or parent-teacher organizations and involves fundraising for arts activities. At other times, it is through the actions of individual parents, who, because they have artistic skills or connections with artists and musicians, can set up after-school programs or arrange for performances and artist visits. Schools have come to rely more and more on parental involvement in order to provide "arts enrichment" activities.[60]

This approach to arts education, along with user-pay programs, can perpetuate inequity in the school system. When a small fee is charged "to help defray expenses" for field trips, school performances and after-school activities, dollar amounts that seem small for affluent parents can add up over the year for low-income parents, even if each individual fee might seem a trivial, if humiliating, reason to ask for help.[61]

As declining enrolments in some schools and the increasing focus on test results lead to cutbacks in arts funding, many educational jurisdictions find that their arts programs are withering away. In rural areas especially, diminishing resources often mean increasing student/teacher ratios, and non-specialist teachers are often teaching music or art — it is not uncommon in some schools to have one teacher teaching both music and gym, for example.[62] In one school I visited, the kindergarten music class, taught by a whistle-blowing gym teacher, consisted of having the children sing along to a CD. It is extremely unlikely that 95 per cent of these children would learn to sing in tune.

But determined, creative arts teachers have sometimes been able to refuse to let unsupportive administrations or lack of funding deter excellence. Chalmers Doane was one such person who, among many other talents, was able to use his powers of persuasion to talk the administration into funding an excellent music program. My own brother, Jack, is another example. He was an elementary music teacher serving multiple schools in a small town in Ontario and for years, he wrote and directed musical plays, based on local issues, which involved every child in the school. Large choirs, backstage crews and huge casts ensured that everyone had a part to play, and rehearsals during school hours allowed the bussed children to participate. Many other teachers helped out, and didn't object when rehearsals encroached on class time. But most significantly, a large number of parents volunteered to help with the productions. These plays became a highlight of the year for the children and the whole community.

Arts programs don't have to be expensive in the early years. Teachers of the arts cost no more than classroom teachers, and collaboration between them can often have surprising results. The annual Plays at Halifax Independent bring out the sometimes hidden artistic talents in everyone, students and teachers alike. And the integration and teaching of the arts contributes to the development of the whole child. Since progressive education is all about teaching the whole child, arts education becomes an integral part. It is not a frill.

Chapter 5
SECOND-LANGUAGE LEARNING

"To learn a language is to have one more window from which to look at the world."

— *Chinese proverb*

Being able to communicate in another language, be it Mandarin, German, Spanish or French, is a wonderful thing. Living in an officially bilingual country, we know that being bilingual will give us an edge in many careers, opening doors for us that would otherwise remain shut. Even better, new research shows that there are intellectual benefits of speaking a second language as well. Like exercise for the body, bilingualism is exercise for the mind and actually increases the size of the language areas of the brain. It gives us improved listening skills, stronger working memories and more cognitive flexibility (multitasking). It deepens our command of our mother tongue and, most comforting for those of us approaching a certain age, bilingualism has been shown to slow dementia.[63] There are many good reasons to want our children to learn a second language!

Every second year the older Middle Schoolers take part in an exchange with a Francophone school.

Since Canada's two official languages are French and English, it is natural that many parents prefer their child to learn the other official language. In English Canada, there have grown a bewildering variety of French as a second language (FSL) programs, ranging from the minimal "core French" to immersion programs that offer full-time French starting in early, middle or late elementary school. Core French programs generally start at Grade 4 in most provinces (except BC, where it starts at Grade 5) and usually involve about thirty to forty minutes per day of French teaching. Immersion programs generally start at 80 to 100 per cent of the day in French, and gradually increase the amount of time in English as children get older.

Canada is a world leader in immersion programs. Early French immersion got its start in the early 1970s as a way to promote bilingualism across the country. After almost fifty years of early immersion, and a focus in Canadian schools on second-language learning, we might expect to have a fully bilingual population, at least among the younger generations. Yet, after all these years, less than one fifth of Canadians reported being able to have a conversation in both English and French.[64]

European countries do so much better than we do at teaching their children second and even third languages. Denmark and other Scandinavian countries top the world list in proficiency in English as a second language — nearly all high school graduates now are functionally bilingual — and they do it by starting English classes at Grade 3. Part of this excellent result is due to the dominance of English in world affairs and the media, but at least some of it can be attributed to the active-learning, communicative style of teaching. Second (and third) language teaching is a priority for such a small country, and they make good use of the time allotted to it. It must be possible to improve our FSL programs so that all our graduates have at least a working knowledge of French.

> Several six- and seven-year-olds are clustered around a large, hand-drawn map of Halifax, clearly labelled in French. Colourful, three-dimensional cardboard houses dot the map, and the children are moving small cut-out photos of themselves along the streets. One child is leading another on a tour ("Regarde, un arbre! Regarde, ma maison!"). Two children's figures are having a conversation: "Où es-tu? Je suis au parc. Où veux-tu aller? Je veux aller au magasin."
>
> At another table, the French teacher is working with a group of three, making a photo story to be videotaped with a voiceover by the children. The children are practising their dialogues, which will accompany the three photos of their figures on the map: starting point, route, and destination. Other children in the class are practising their dialogues, or finishing up various props for

the map. The general conversational hum includes many French words and phrases.

In the Halifax Independent School elementary school, the whole-school theme is integrated as much as possible into the core French classes that children start taking three times per week from the age of five. The scenario described above was done during the Nova Scotia theme year, when the class was studying neighbourhoods. The opportunity to work and play with the model of Halifax reinforced some of the concepts of neighbourhood (parks, community centres, fire stations, etc.) while introducing new French words and structures. At the same time, the children were learning about maps, directions and other geographical concepts that are covered in the theme class.

One year, during the Oceans theme, the ten- and eleven-year-olds invented their own species of fish in French class. Then students made multimedia paintings of their inventions and created personalities to go along with them. They wrote descriptions in French using structures that included "Je m'appelle . . . Je suis____ et _____ et très _____ (fill in with adjectives). J'aime manger les . . ." To extend this, they later did interviews with each other, with each child playing the role of interviewer and interviewee. The same year, the eight- and nine-year-olds made stuffed, cut-out paper models of the shoreline creature they were studying in theme, and wrote structured poems in French about them. By using in French class what they had learned in theme about fish or other sea creatures, students are getting extra reinforcement. In addition, the French teacher can capitalize on the children's interest in what they are studying, and harness that motivation to produce work the children can then display at their Fair presentations.

This is an example of a project-based or an active learning, communicative approach to language teaching. The children are actively engaged in working on a project for which real communication is required. Their learning in French is integrated into what they are doing in the rest of their school day.

IS AN EARLY START BETTER?

There has been a great deal of money and research put into expanding and improving immersion programs over the past fifty years. One of the few educational areas that has escaped cutbacks is early French immersion, which starts in kindergarten or Grade 1. In fact, it has experienced huge growth (increasing 12 per cent between 2006 and 2013), while overall student enrolment has been declining. Lotteries or long parent line-ups decide who can get in, as the demand generally outstrips the supply. If all children could take early immersion (or even middle or late immersion), we might be able to achieve results similar to the Scandinavian second language programs — but there are reasons why that will not happen with the current system.

I used to be a firm believer in early immersion, and I would have enrolled my own children in it, had it been possible. But I've changed my mind. My years of teaching and a Master's of Education in second language instruction have given me a new perspective. Early French immersion, although it can have excellent results for the children who stay in the program until the end of high school, may not be the best way for children to learn a second language.

The belief that young children absorb new languages effortlessly is one of the fundamental assumptions behind the introduction of early immersion programs. Another assumption, based on the critical period hypothesis in second language learning, is that there is an optimum age for second language learning, which is essentially over by puberty. After that age, the theory goes, speakers may become fluent in a second language, but they will never have a native-like accent. However, in the last twenty years, this hypothesis has been questioned, and problems with the methodology of some of the earlier research studies have been pointed out.[65] There is a considerable body of research that points out older learners' "learning effectiveness." Older students, with their knowledge of English grammar, ability to read in their mother tongue and better organizational skills, are actually more efficient language learners than younger children.[66] We also know now that it is not so effortless for younger learners to learn a second language as it may appear.

I have also seen that, because of their limited French skills, students in the early years of immersion who are expected to speak only French in the classroom simply do not speak as much as those studying in their mother tongue. Inevitably this affects their verbal development and confidence as they grow. By contrast, Halifax Independent School aims to develop children's deeper mother tongue language skills from an early age, and so we find very young children are discussing complex issues, solving problems, negotiating and explaining concepts to each other. This is very important for their intellectual development. The lag in early immersion students' ability to communicate holds teachers back from the kind of deeper discussions involved in active learning, and it lasts throughout elementary school.

Another problem with early immersion is the "streaming" effect. In practice, most early immersion programs have become quite elitist, basically "free private schools within the public school system."[67] The socio-economic level of immersion students is considerably higher than in English programs. In addition, access to programs is very spotty, with rural areas often offering no immersion programs at all. And, although the conventional wisdom is that early immersion is suitable for all students,[68] the reality is that children whose first language is not English and those with various behavioural, intellectual or socio-economic challenges are often discouraged from enrolling or advised to leave the program after a few years. This is partly because there is little French language resource help for them. Because of all this, the more academically inclined children tend to end up in early immersion, resulting in a type of streaming that has worse academic outcomes for all students, but especially for the English stream.[69]

By Grade 6, about 20 per cent of the original immersion entrants have dropped out of early immersion, primarily boys, students from lower socio-economic classes and children with special needs, thus accentuating the streaming effect.[70] Many immersion-oriented parents frankly admit that where there is a choice, why would they risk putting their children in the English stream where they will be lumped in with more behaviourally and academically challenged students?

Because there is a shortage of trained, native-speaking French teachers in Canada, French immersion classes are often taught either by non-native speakers (sometimes with less than perfect accents and usage) or native speakers with unconventional training. This shortage, and the restricted language skills that early-immersion students possess in their second language, contributes to the more traditional teaching style that is often found in early immersion classes. It is just very difficult to do the in-depth discussion required by inquiry or theme-based classes when students do not have the language skills to express themselves.

What are the results of all those early years of French language learning? Is early immersion fulfilling its promise? Not exactly — studies are divided on whether students' French proficiency at the end of high school is better for those who started early or those who took late immersion programs (either Grade 4 or 7).[71] Numerous studies have compared results, and although most report early gains in French proficiency for early immersion over late or middle immersion, many report that those differences are negligible by the time students graduate.[72]

Finally, 50 per cent of students from both early immersion and late immersion drop out of bilingual programs when they get to high school, chiefly because they are worried about the negative impact on their marks. If we have universities that prioritize marks over all other indicators when looking at acceptance, this will continue to be a problem.

Given the considerations listed above, along with the lack of conclusive proof that early immersion is substantially better at creating bilingualism, we need alternatives that are more cost effective, equitable and in line with the development of every child.

> In 2008, the New Brunswick Education Minister started a firestorm of controversy by declaring that bilingualism would become an expectation for all, instead of an option for the few. He proposed the elimination of early French immersion in favour of middle immersion for all children starting in Grade 5.
>
> A report by two researchers (Croll and Lee)[73] found that the early immersion programs in New Brunswick were not meeting their FSL objectives, that there was a high drop-out rate and that there were negative effects on the majority who were not in French immersion. The reaction to the minister's decision took observers by surprise, with demonstrations, public forums that descended into hooting and hollering and blogs such as the one entitled, "Immersion Delayed is Immersion Denied." There were public debates between people like Douglas Willms, who claimed that "school choice is not a right

when it has a negative effect on the educational provision of other children,"[74] and Joseph Dicks, who argued that early immersion would have better results and be more inclusive if there were more supports in place for children who struggle.[75]

The public outcry culminated in a court challenge in which the education minister was ordered to make a revised decision after hearing from citizens and organized groups. The result was a plan that seemed to get the approval of many: early immersion would start in Grade 3, with an alternate program called "English prime," which would gradually increase French instruction and lead to late immersion in Grade 6 or a continuation of English prime. Everyone would have access to the same courses in Grades 11 and 12.

Grades	New Brunswick Education Program Options	
K-2	English Prime with learning experiences to introduce French language and culture	
3	English Prime with learning experiences to introduce French language and culture	
4	English Prime with Pre-Intensive French	
5	English Prime with Intensive French	French Immersion
6-10	English Prime with Post-Intensive French	
11-12	Blended High School Program	Late French Immersion

OTHER OPTIONS

There are other varieties of immersion programs that start later — middle immersion, which starts in either Grade 4 or 5, and late immersion, which starts in Grade 6 or 7. Some school boards offer a choice of immersion programs; some offer just one variant or none at all. Generally, later immersion programs start with an intensive 100 per cent French *bain linguistique* for several months, and then settle into around fifty-fifty French-English, with some subjects taught entirely in French and others in English.

Often, these later immersion programs attract students who are motivated and confident in their second-language abilities. This may be one reason that their French proficiency rivals that of early immersion by the end of high school. Another reason may be that there is an advantage to children who learn to read in their mother tongue before learning a second language. It is especially true for minority language children in Canada; middle or late immersion is preferable for them.[76] UNESCO, which looks at education around the world, has long recognized the need for mother-tongue instruction in developing countries before children learn the official language (often English) as a second language in school. In 2010 it stated, "fluency and literacy in the mother tongue lay a cognitive and linguistic foundation for learning additional languages. When children receive formal instruction in their first language throughout primary school and then gradually transition to academic learning in the second language, they learn the second language quickly."[77] There is a great deal of other research that confirms that "reading ability [in the mother tongue] facilitates the learning of a second language."[78]

> While the upper elementary classes are "discovering the world" in their theme classes, in French class they are also learning about the world map and naming countries and continents in French. They learn about gendered nouns (le Canada), about comparative language such as "plus petit," and about location: "proche de." While working on their French maps, they are reinforcing their knowledge of where countries are in the world. One class created a true/false quiz that they could give to another class that involved statements such as: "'Le Canada est un petit pays en Antarctique' — vrai ou faux?" and "La Russie est la plus grande pays du monde."

> While working on writing the questions, the issue of how to express "proche de" came up, and Tania was able to explain the use of du, de la and des to children who were ready to hear it, and who began using it immediately. The novelty of giving a quiz to their classmates was very motivating for the children, as was recording their statements on the mini voice recorders. Doing these activities integrated work on sentence structure, introduced new grammar ideas and solidified students' geographical sense. It is excellent preparation for their upcoming study of countries in "la Francophonie."

The majority of students in Canada learn French in core programs, usually thirty to forty minute periods three or four times per week starting at Grade 4 or 5. Research shows that children do not gain in French proficiency for starting core French earlier. So, when resources are limited, it makes sense to concentrate core French in the intermediate years (Grades 5 to 8). The same research also recommends a collaborative, project-based approach, with longer blocks of time allotted so that the language can be integrated into the experiential learning. Letting the students be more involved in planning what they want to learn and giving them more opportunities to collaborate means more talking, and genuine communication is key to good language learning.[79]

> **La Crèmerie**
> At Halifax Independent School, some Friday mornings see one class put on a bake sale, to which all children and teachers are invited. The class raises money for something they can all agree on — a charity, a class pet or some new equipment for the classroom.
> One Friday every second year, all of that changes when the six- and seven- year olds invite the rest of the school to attend "La Crèmerie" (a French-language ice cream parlour). Classes troop

through in fifteen-minute intervals, greeted by the hosts singing a little jingle entitled "Vive Crème Glacée." The customers line up at the counter, order one of the four flavours on offer (in French, of course) as well as toppings. They are served by the host children, who engage in dialogue such as "Vous désirez?" and "Un dollar, s'il vous plaît." While the visiting class enjoys their ice cream, the hosts circulate, politely inquiring, "Ça va bien?"

This event is the end result of a lot of preparation on the part of all the children in the school, and is highly anticipated. The six- and seven-year-olds learn language around offering and questioning, and polite greetings and farewells. They learn how to express preferences, and to describe the different ice cream flavours and toppings. Then, they visit each classroom in the school, asking how many people like each flavour of ice cream and topping, and use this to determine the menu. This is excellent French number practice. They record their survey results on a large graph, which is later displayed for all to see. The hosts design and make menus, create decorations that show their ideal ice cream cones and make special serving caps to be worn on the day. The rest of the school practises ordering ice cream, and the politeness vocabulary that goes with it.

After the event is over and the money counted (all proceeds go toward buying French supplies), the children are happy to relive the event by creating cartoons showing the conversations they had while selling "crème glacée" at La Crèmerie. They happily take home their caps, the menus they made and their beautifully decorated ice cream cones.

An interesting variation of core French is "intensive French," such as that offered in BC at Grade 6, where the first half of the year is completely in French (except for math) and then there is sixty minutes of French per day in the second half of the year, in which communication

Middles serving ice cream at "La Crèmerie."

is paramount. Research is promising for this intensive French, where longer blocks of time are allotted and where a "project-based approach" is used. Perhaps because the children can feel more immersed in the language, because the project captures their interest more than learning language in isolation or because they are given more autonomy over their learning, outcomes tend to be better than regular core French for this type of approach. Even though these students are not doing English language arts for half the school year, their English outcomes are as good as children in English programs.[80] Promising results have been found for this program, with intensive French students actually achieving what researchers call "spontaneous communication" after one year. Core French students seldom achieve this level.[81]

When Halifax Independent School started its middle school, it introduced "extended core French," starting in Grade 6, where students had science or social studies in French in addition to French language classes. Again, learning a subject and the language at the same time had the effect of reinforcing the other, and the "project-based" approach was more interesting for the students. However, when we started the program, we had hoped that late immersion programs would be offered in the junior high schools within the inner city of Halifax where most of our students lived. That never happened, so, although the program worked well for some students, when they graduated the local high schools they went to didn't know what to do with them. Our students were not eligible for high school immersion programs because they had not come from early immersion, and there was no provision for late immersion students. Having to then revert back to the core French programs in high school was discouraging, and when it became obvious that late immersion was not going to happen in inner Halifax, the extended core French was dropped.

    Another problem that I observed with the extended core French at Halifax Independent School was that we had perhaps left its introduction a little late, especially after the start of middle school was changed to Grade 7. By that age, many children are self-conscious, and less likely to take risks in front of their peers — if they are unsure about their pronunciation and usage of French, they will be less likely to speak, and therefore slower to learn the language. Starting extended core French at Grade 5 or even earlier would build students' confidence before they reach the awkwardness of puberty and may result in better fluency and accent.

THE ROAD TO BETTER SECOND LANGUAGE LEARNING

Early immersion, even after fifty years, is still not universally available, and where it is offered, the graduates are likely to be from the highest socio-economic levels, white and female. Early immersion sucks up a huge share of the resources (trained, native-speaking teachers) that could be used elsewhere, and this compounds its negative effect on the non-immersion programs.

Knowledge of French gives adults a leg up getting jobs, so shouldn't we as a country be trying to give every child the same chances? My own children could not benefit from early immersion because we lived in a rural area where it was not offered. Now, when I pick up my granddaughters from their lovely early immersion program in downtown Toronto, I can't help but notice that most of the immigrant students in the school are concentrated in the English program. Is it not time that we refocus energies on making bilingualism possible for all children, instead of just the few?

New Brunswick's goal of bilingualism for all, instead of just for the few, could be an objective for the whole country. Their English Prime stream offers a good starting model for educational reform, but I would suggest it would be even better if every child could start immersion in Grade 6. Every child would do pre-intensive French in Grade 4, intensive French in Grade 5, late immersion in Grades 6 to 10 (50 per cent French and English) and a blended high school program for Grades 11 and 12. In high school, students could choose to take more or fewer French classes, and if they take enough, have the option of graduating with a bilingual certificate. The intensive French in elementary school and the late immersion in middle school would all be project-, inquiry- or theme-based, and French would be taught in a way that emphasizes spoken communication initially. This would lead to a very high rate of functionally bilingual graduates who would have the potential, with further study or exposure, to achieve full bilingualism.

Research shows the results of early immersion have not been nearly as good as one would expect, given all the extra years that children are learning French. In addition, in the early years of immersion, children may lose out on valuable time learning to express more abstract concepts in their own language. Delaying the start of immersion capitalizes on the "learning effectiveness" of the older learner and allows children to learn to read in the mother tongue before starting second-language learning. This appears to benefit all children, but especially minority language students learning more than one language at a time. With more education and research about the benefits of delaying immersion programs to later in elementary, many parents may decide that it would actually be better for their children educationally.

If each province had a universal French second language program similar to the one I described, there would be one less variable that parents have to worry about when choosing a school for their children. If all children followed such a plan, they could all go to their neighbourhood school (less bussing!), and from Grade 4 on, they would be taught by the former early immersion teachers, who are no longer needed in the earlier grades. There would be resource help for all children who need it in French, but perhaps there would be less need, because by that time almost all the children would be reading comfortably in English.

Parents at Halifax Independent have made the choice to educate their children in English. Some of those children

Middle schoolers and their Quebec guests paint a mural in the back stairwell of the school.

started out in early French immersion but were part of the 20 per cent who, for various reasons, didn't thrive in the program. Their parents and many other Halifax Independent parents might be very happy to give their children a chance at late immersion or intensive French in middle school if the public high schools offered a blended immersion program. If that happened, it wouldn't be surprising to see a new version of extended core resurface.

I know that early immersion is not going anywhere soon — it is so entrenched and works well for many children. However, I continue to believe that the excellent academic and French proficiency results shown by intensive French and late immersion hold a lot of promise for French teaching in Canada.

Chapter 6
THE WHOLE CHILD: SOCIO-EMOTIONAL LEARNING

"Our job is not to toughen our children up to face a cruel and heartless world. Our job is to raise children who will make the world a little less cruel and heartless."

— L.R. Knost

There are two things that I believe to be true about almost all children: they want the approval of the significant adults in their lives and they are always learning from situations, although not necessarily what we want or expect them to.

Getting adult approval is not always easy for children — they have irresistible impulses that get in the way, and sometimes their significant adults are very difficult to please. It's a fact of life that our children are not always angels. I have a vivid childhood memory of cramming a whole packet of gum into my mouth in order to destroy the evidence of a crime — shoplifting from Shoppers' City — because I was sure the police would be knocking on my door any minute. I must have learned something from this event, since I did not repeat it.

Schools have the job, along with parents, of passing along values and preparing children to take part in society. That includes sometimes having to deal with social problems. A few years back, when Halifax Independent School was beginning to grow more quickly, we were presented with a puzzling situation. Once in a while, children would report that something was missing from their lunchboxes, some Dunkaroos here, a packet of Cheestrings there. At first we thought it was just children being careless, but after a few weeks an obvious pattern emerged. Everyone was talking about it — who could the mystery thief be? After some digging, the teachers discovered that it was Tamara, a spirited eight-year-old who had been helping herself to various prepackaged snacks from other children's lunches.

In some schools she would be sent to the principal to receive a stern lecture about how stealing is wrong, in fact illegal. Her parents would be called and she would get an appropriate punishment. Instead, her classroom teacher sat down alone with her for a chat. At first Tamara was stubborn, resentful and defiant, and denied that she was the culprit. After some time (and undeniable evidence), she broke down and admitted that she took the snacks because her parents never gave her anything prepackaged, and she was longing to be like everyone else. As it happened, her homemade lunches and baked goods were the envy of the teachers. When her parents were included in the discussion, it ranged from why they don't give her prepackaged snacks to the lack of trust the other children feel toward Tamara now. The consequence that was decided involved not just using her allowance to pay back the children whose snacks she had taken, but writing notes to each one explaining what she had done and apologizing for it.

I use this as an example of how a school that puts a priority on socio-emotional learning handles problems.

Making a display for Fair.

In many schools, when a defiant, guilty child is sent to the principal's office, the priority is to punish them. In this case, seldom does the principal get beyond the defiance, and sometimes it escalates into swearing, throwing things and even physical attacks. It is not uncommon for a relatively minor problem to result in a child being removed from school. What would Tamara have learned if she had been treated this way? She would have learned that stealing is wrong, a strong value in our society — but then, she already knew that. Other lessons she might have learned: don't get caught, keep your emotions in check, don't talk about your problems and your classmates won't like you because of what you have done.

What did Tamara actually learn from the stealing incident? She learned that adults respect and care about her, problems can be solved constructively and relationships can be repaired. She and the other children involved learned about a proactive way of solving problems, a model they may use themselves in the future. But she also learned in a visceral and personalized way that stealing is not a socially acceptable way of behaving.

Socio-emotional learning is not just about solving social problems; it is also about feeling respected and being respectful of others in a genuine way. It is about creating the conditions for happiness, learning about cooperation and competition and about children understanding that they have a say over what happens to them and the world around them. It is about the whole child.

When Tamara was taking snacks from her classmates' lunchboxes, she was feeling envious, marginalized and "different." When she heard that everyone was looking for the "thief," she became worried about being caught, and when she was finally found out, she thought her friends wouldn't like her anymore. She was not a happy child during this time.

A child who is focused on something else cannot concentrate on schoolwork. Children live intensely in the moment, and things that an adult might not consider a crisis can loom large to children. Worry about not being invited to a birthday party, being excluded from a game or having an unresolved argument with a friend can all be more important to a child than the lesson of the day. An unhappy child will not be able to fully concentrate and won't benefit from whatever learning situation they are in.

Teachers know from day-to-day experience that children who feel respected and are happy, who have strong self-esteem and who have the ability to cooperate and negotiate social situations are better equipped for academic learning than those who don't. We adults know that this emotional intelligence is important for life beyond school as well. The key issue here, then, is how schools can teach and model social skills and values so that all children will have that foundation for empathy and emotional learning. If we truly want an education system that will prepare children for the challenges of the future, these skills are far from "frills."

Although the formal curriculum of many schools recognizes the importance of these soft skills, the reality is that even when they are explicitly taught (and often they aren't) the children may be learning something quite different. What children actually learn is often described as the "hidden curriculum," and this chapter will deal with how Halifax Independent aligns the explicit curriculum with the hidden curriculum, while teaching social skills and values.

THE HIDDEN CURRICULUM

What Tamara and her friends learned from the stealing incident was in line with what Halifax Independent School explicitly teaches. But every school teaches values. In schools where they are not taught explicitly, values, habits and social skills are taught by example. Some of this implicit teaching happens informally in the playground culture, where it often evolves without teachers' awareness. Another large part of it is transmitted through the structure of the school, and the way the teachers interact with the students and each other. In many ways, this hidden curriculum — that is, everything the children learn that is not explicitly taught — is a far deeper influence than the formal curriculum.

In rhetoric if not reality, educators have begun to recognize the power of this hidden curriculum, and it is often referred to as the "climate" of the school. At Halifax Independent, teachers, parents and students collaborated over the years to develop the philosophy, and then the policies, to create a climate that put a priority on socio-emotional learning.

But many schools do not take the time and conscious effort to bring the hidden curriculum of a school in line with the values and social skills it wants students to learn.

Even when social skills and values are taught explicitly, reality trumps rhetoric — saying stuff is often not enough to counteract the hidden messaging. When I taught in Britain, for example, the school's formal rhetoric was about the benefits of sharing and cooperating, and school assemblies were held on the topic, but the daily reality in the classroom was that children were pitted against each other in a highly competitive, hierarchical, marks-driven culture. The rhetoric was cooperation, but the reality was that everyone was on their own.

Making sure children learn what we want them to from the hidden curriculum can be a time-consuming process. It took time initially for her teacher to sit down with Tamara, to probe enough to get past her defiance and to work with the parents and other children to develop an appropriate consequence. If the teacher had simply sent the child to the principal to be "disciplined," it may have initially taken less time, but could have pushed the problem underground where it could resurface later. Making the effort to develop a school climate collaboratively and then implementing it is worth it.

A HAPPY CHILD

> *"We understand that a happy child learns best and that each child learns and develops in many different ways."*
> — *Halifax Independent School website*[82]

With the trend toward smaller families and more mobility in parental employment leading to fewer community ties, schools today play a larger role in the emotional lives of children than they did forty years ago. A school can provide extra support for those times in a child's life when external events create a crisis. And for children who come from troubled homes or backgrounds, it is more important than ever that schools are seen as safe, happy places.

One prerequisite for a child's happiness is a healthy, robust sense of self. Children who are confident in their abilities can take the risks associated with learning (if you think you will not succeed, why waste the effort?), and will be more inclined to work hard and challenge themselves, which means they are more likely to experience greater academic success. Research has found a positive correlation between self-esteem and academic success, even recognizing the bidirectional nature of the relationship (good academic performance also has an impact on self-esteem).[83]

Nevertheless, self-esteem has had some bad press recently. Books like *The Triple Package*[84] by Amy Chua and Jed Rubenfeld warn parents that too much praise creates entitlement. Why would children work hard if they are praised for everything?

It is true that indiscriminate praise can undermine self-esteem. Children can quickly tell when praise is not deserved and may begin to doubt its meaning. Next, they may question whether anything they do is praiseworthy, which undermines the value of their real accomplishments. However, a lack of praise when a child has tried hard can also be devastating. Not all children will continue to try hard if they feel they have failed, or if no one has appreciated the effort they have made. Many will become discouraged and give up trying.

Knowing when and how to praise is a skill that good teachers possess, and parents can learn it too. The purpose of praise is to send a signal that students are going in the right direction, and to acknowledge effort — in other words, to encourage them. But it should only be given when it is actually deserved: when a good teacher is confronted with a slapdash effort from someone she knows can do better, she will question it. Children need to develop a healthy, realistic sense of their own worth, to better enable them to accept and learn from constructive feedback.

One of the striking findings of the international PISA tests recognizes that practice and hard work are key to success, and that students' beliefs in their control over their own success is paramount.

Three decades of research by Carol Dweck and others has shown that students with what she calls a "growth mindset," who believe that working hard can make them smarter, do better academically than those with a "fixed mindset," who believe that abilities are innate and unchangeable. One child I taught had been told how smart she was so often that she felt she never had to work at anything. It was true that she was very good at mathematics, but her belief in her innate intelligence meant that she seldom exerted any effort, and thus produced a lot of mediocre work that was much less than she was capable of. Children with that kind of fixed mindset are vulnerable to blows to their self-esteem when they encounter work that really challenges them. Of even greater concern are children who believe they don't have what it takes to succeed, and this fixed mindset may stop them from even trying.

If the climate of the school is positive and nurturing, if mutual respect is the goal and if students are rewarded with judicious praise for hard work, they will develop growth mindsets and their self-esteem will flourish. They are more likely to be happy. Unfortunately, report cards or test results that record failure (and keep in mind that for some children, failure can be anything less than an A or equivalent) can be devastating to many of them. This is especially true in the later elementary years, from ages eight to eleven, when children are beginning to be aware of and compare themselves to their peer group. But more importantly, sending the implicit message that doing well on report cards or tests is the main goal of education becomes part of the hidden curriculum. This can undermine the motivation of many children, and prevent them from seeing the importance of effort.

Chapter 7 details a method of authentic assessment that does not involve report cards or tests until the middle or high school years. It takes into account individual differences, strengths and weaknesses, and compares students only with themselves — are they doing better or worse than the last time? Have they been putting in the effort that is required to achieve what is expected? Without the necessity to get "good" marks on a report card, children are given permission to take more chances with their learning. Then, when an experiment, a project or a challenge does not work out, the result can be treated as a learning opportunity. Is it because of a random event, a lack of hard work or poor design? The children, although they take responsibility for the bad result, will not see it as their failure as a human being. They will be more likely to see the benefits of effort.

Children notice when other children can do things they cannot do. Comparison with peers is constant and unavoidable — whether it is speed in running or in arithmetic. But the important thing is what a child learns from comparisons. Learning to read later, difficulties grasping math concepts or illegible spelling can all lead to a student questioning her self-worth. In these cases, extra help from teachers and parents, an acknowledgement that the student is experiencing difficulty and an emphasis on all the things she does well go a long way to mitigating the effects. Frank discussions in the classroom about strengths and weaknesses also help students feel that they are not alone, as well as emphasizing the importance of hard work — both to excel at what you do well, and to improve on your weaknesses. Again, this will help the development of a "growth mindset" in children.

A child who feels that no one expects much from him will probably fulfill that expectation, and that will fuel his lack of self-esteem. When a teacher (or parent) expects, and helps, children to do work that they can be proud of, their self-esteem rises, and they will be more willing to take chances the next time. It is a virtuous circle and reinforces the idea that all children are respected and appreciated.

CREATING A CULTURE OF RESPECT

> *"All I really need to know I learned in kindergarten. Share everything. Play fair. Don't hit people. Put things back where you found them. Clean up your own mess. Don't take things that aren't yours. Say you're sorry when you hurt somebody."*
> *— Robert Fulghum* [85]

The twenty-first century requires much more of its citizens in terms of social skills and emotional intelligence than these simple values. It is important that children continue to learn these skills throughout their school life, through both their school's hidden and explicit curriculum.

A culture of mutual respect is fundamental to creating

the conditions for teaching emotional intelligence. Respect in a school community is multi-faceted: respect for one's self, for one's peers, mutual respect between adults and children in the community and respect for those outside the community. Children who feel respected are more likely to respect others in return.

Most provinces have put all the right words into their educational mission statements: anti-bullying and cyber-bullying laws and policies are ubiquitous in Canada now. Yet after-the-fact curricula and policies to address hot issues often fail because they are treating the symptoms and not the cause. Wearing pink shirts for a day or organizing anti-bullying workshops are nice, but these events do little to address underlying problems. These initiatives advocate respect without ensuring that it is shared in all directions. When children don't learn about healthy relationships from a very early age, they will find it difficult to handle bullying when it happens. It is far more effective for a school to develop a climate that has respect at the very core, and which comes from both teachers and students.

Teachers and principals in Canada are beginning to recognize this. In Nova Scotia, the "Speak Up" program recognizes the importance of relationships and developing mutual respect from an early age. Teachers are being trained in "restorative approaches,"[86] which include many of the social skills and school climate issues that could go a long way to making bullying a thing of the past. Most provinces now have similar programs. However, I fear that the enormous pressure that teachers are under to raise test scores will interfere with the implementation of programs such as these, so it is essential that as parents and teachers, we support and encourage these initiatives.

What does a school look like where mutual respect is practised?

First, self-respect and respect for others is taught both explicitly and by example from the earliest years. Self-respect is bound up in self-esteem. Children need to and can learn that they have rights, and how to stand up for those rights without infringing on the rights of others. This is what kindergarten used to be about, and what still needs to be taught explicitly. From the earliest age, specific language can be taught to give children the tools to tell each other when they feel that boundaries are being breached ("I feel hurt/sad when you . . ."). By phrasing these sentiments in "I" messages (instead of the blaming "you did that"), children learn to send the message to each other that it is the behaviour that is problematic, not the other child. Children learn that every human being deserves our respect, even when their behaviour may be a problem. And this needs to be modelled constantly by the teachers, parents and older children. Children then learn that others' basic respect for them never wavers and that the expectation is that they will behave in the same way to their peers.

For the youngest children, the focus is on teaching about rights and responsibilities over their own bodies and property ("I don't like it when you touch me there"), but as they get older, they learn about many other rights and responsibilities (privacy, ideologies, etc.). Empathy and appreciation for people who have different beliefs, cultures or appearances can be taught explicitly. Schools that teach about different religions and cultures invite discussion about a diversity of views, especially when these units involve the community and families.

Second, the hidden curriculum of a school should promote respect. When looking at the structure of a school, how the teachers and administrators interact with each other reveals a lot. Too much deference or fear of authority among teachers is a bad sign, as is unhappiness, stress or negativity toward other staff members. In the school in which I taught in Britain, teachers were often fearful of authority figures, whether it was the department head who would be evaluating them, the principal who may be concerned about exam results or education department inspectors making a spot visit. When the teachers pass this on to the children, as can happen especially when exam time approaches, they are contributing to a culture of fear.

A school that practises true respect does not need fear or hierarchy to shore it up. When teachers feel supported and respected, they look on authority figures as sources of help, inspiration or advice. At Halifax Independent School, no one has a title — all teachers, administrators and parents are known by their first names. Some visitors to the school looked askance at this practice and asked me, "How do you maintain the respect of students for their teachers when they call them by their first names?" The answer is simple: in a culture where everyone is respected, regardless of status or age, titles are not necessary. In fact, titles promote the idea that there is a hierarchy of respect and that adults are more worthy of it than children.

The setup of the various classrooms in a school is an indicator of how the teacher interacts with the students and the school's culture of respect. A teacher who spends most of her time at the front of the classroom, either at the board or seated at her desk, is implicitly taking on the role of authority and disseminator of knowledge (vertical teaching). Children naturally feel that they are less important, less deserving of respect. A teacher whose desk is tucked away somewhere in the classroom, and who spends most of her time sitting with groups of children or moving about, reflects the role of the teacher in the class as a fellow learner, as a facilitator of learning. This "horizontal" teaching style means that teachers gain a relationship with their students based on mutual respect and genuine appreciation. A child who knows that she is respected will in turn have respect for those around her.

> **Sticks and stones may break my bones,
> But names will always hurt me.**
> This slogan, on a small poster in the lunchroom of the school when I started there, was often referred to at the whole-school Meeting. It led to the adoption of one of the few absolute rules at the school that has endured to this day: No calling anyone by any name other than their actual name.
>   It acknowledges that name-calling actually can hurt you as much as a physical hit, and that emotional well-being is as important as physical and intellectual well-being. By constantly being reminded of this rule, the children internalize a baseline of respect for themselves and others that contributes to the overall climate of respect.

Other observable indicators are the way the teachers interact with their students and the existence of policies that encourage communication and sharing between families and teachers. Where a climate of respect has been created, teachers will listen to the children with genuine interest and respond to their questions and concerns with the same respect they would show another adult. They will show a knowledge and appreciation of the students' family background, and will welcome parents' insight into their child's school life.

Schools in which the hidden curriculum and the explicit curriculum are aligned and which truly promote mutual respect possess the foundation for excellent values and social skills education.

CONFLICT RESOLUTION

> Two six-year-olds, Sally and Amir, are running around the playground when suddenly shrieks are heard, and the two are observed locked in a struggle over a stick. Amir has almost succeeded in wresting it from Sally when the teacher intervenes, grabs the stick and holds it in the air.
> Teacher (in a firm voice): "Now then, you two, who had this first?"
> Sally and Amir (in unison): "I did!"
> Teacher: "That's not possible: once more, who had it first?"
> Amir: "It was my stick!"
> Sally: "Well, he gave it to me."
> Teacher: "So why are you fighting over it?"
> Amir: "I did not give it to her!"
> Teacher: "Sally, is that true?"
> Sally: "Yeeees, but . . ."
> Teacher: "All right then, here you go, Amir, take your stick. And Sally, what can you say?"
> Sally: "Well, SORRY, but . . ."
> Teacher: "Off you go, and if I see you two fighting over that stick again, I will take it away from both of you!"
> The two children wander off, Amir aimlessly swinging the stick. Sally stomps off, but as soon as the teacher's attention is elsewhere, she sticks her foot out and trips Amir.

Sadly, conflicts are part of life — and if mishandled, they can lead to much unhappiness and strife for a child. The teacher in the example above probably thinks she has dealt with the problem "fairly" and expects it to go away. At least she has dealt with it: playground conflicts can often be "under the radar" of the teachers. However, she has also just reinforced the hidden curriculum lesson that "as long as we don't get into trouble it's okay." She has missed an opportunity to model problem solving that allows the children to work out a solution.

Many of us grew up with this kind of conflict resolution. But it does not deal with the underlying emotions, which will inevitably crop up again if they are not expressed. More seriously, the adult is taking away from the children the experience of working through their own problems, and this deprives them of an opportunity to learn skills that are vital to the development of emotional intelligence.

Resolving conflicts in a respectful, empathic way should be a priority for all schools, and an integral part of creating a positive school climate. A peer mediator program is a good start. But it is not enough to train a few students in the techniques so that they can be peer mediators; all children need to learn the language of conflict resolution and practise the listening skills that are necessary to solve their own problems without teacher intervention. A school that is serious about promoting social skills will likely display some evidence of it in the children's work. This does not include prefabricated slogans or bulletin board displays about respect, but actual evidence that the children themselves are actively working on solving conflicts and promoting mutual esteem.

When someone hurts them either physically or verbally, children need the vocabulary to express their feelings. However, if feelings are too hurt for children to deal with the situation on their own, they need to know to ask for teacher or peer mediator help. Asking for help from a teacher is not considered "telling on" someone; indeed, it is the right thing to do, especially if there is any physical or verbal hurting going on.

THE WHOLE CHILD: SOCIO-EMOTIONAL LEARNING 171

Peer mediators help out on the playground.

All schools have to deal with conflict. The way the teachers deal with it — by taking the children involved aside to a quiet space, and following basic conflict resolution techniques to let each child have their say and help them resolve the problem — is key to establishing the climate of respect. Modelling this type of conflict resolution should not be looked upon as lost academic time, but as an essential learning opportunity.

This is something I had to learn when I started at Halifax Independent. The culture of the school showed me a way of handling problems that did not involve assigning blame for starting disputes. When I first began to help children solve their problems with each other by allowing them each to tell the story from the beginning, it almost seemed like a miracle how easily we reached a resolution. When all sides felt heard and respected, apologies and solutions often arose spontaneously, without the teacher having to force them. It was one of the first lessons I learned at Halifax Independent.

When students observe teachers resolving conflicts and begin to learn how to handle issues themselves, it becomes part of the culture of the school. Some children will show a natural affinity for or interest in resolving conflicts, and when they are old enough, they can be invited to become part of the peer mediator team. They will receive extra training that will involve role playing, practising framing questions in a non-judgmental fashion, learning about the roadblocks to communication and memorizing the steps of conflict mediation.

> Six-year-olds Sally and Amir are chasing each other around the play structure. They seem to be having fun, but suddenly shrieks are heard and they are observed locked in battle: Sally is clutching Amir's coat, while he is attempting to wrest a stick from her hand. The playground monitor separates the two, asks them to cool down and calls over Graeme, an older boy wearing a blue sash.
>
> "Do you need a peer mediator?" he asks the two. Sally nods slowly, while Amir, still crying, kicks the gravel with his foot. The monitor melts away, while Graeme leads the children to a quiet corner. He asks Amir, "Are you willing to try to work this out?"
>
> This time Amir, wiping the tears from his face, says reluctantly, "Okay."
>
> Graeme asks Sally if she would like to tell what happened. "We were playing Lost in Space, and I was the spaceship commander and we were fighting aliens. I had the magic light sabre . . ."
>
> "But I had it first!" interrupts Amir.
>
> "Remember the rules of mediation: no interrupting," Graeme says.
>
> "But I am the Commander!" interjected Sally, "It is my job to protect the spaceship! I was just zapping the aliens with the light sabre, and Amir started trying to grab it from me. So I ran away."
>
> Graeme: "Okay, so how did you feel when that happened?"

> Sally: "Really bad."
> Graeme: "Now, Amir, it is your turn to tell what happened."
> Amir: "Well, like Sally said, except that I got the stick from the bushes and I had it. Then when the aliens attacked, she just grabbed it from me and said that she had to fight the aliens because she is the Commander."
> Graeme: "How did that make you feel?"
> Amir: "I was really mad!"
> Graeme: "So it sounds like you both feel pretty bad about this! Sally, can you think of anything you could have done differently?"
> Sally: "Well, I guess I could have asked Amir for the stick."
> Graeme: "Amir? What could you have done differently?"
> Amir: "I guess I didn't need to try to grab it from her."
> Graeme: "Okay, how do you think you could solve this problem?"
> Amir: "Well, sorry, Sally. How about you get the stick to fight the aliens, and then it will be my turn to be the Commander, and I can have the stick?"
> Sally: "Okay. That sounds like a good idea. I'm sorry I just grabbed the stick."
> Graeme: "Are you both okay with Amir's idea?"
> Amir and Sally: "Yes. Can we go play now?"
> Graeme: "Here's the stick, Sally. Good mediation, you two!"
> Amir and Sally scamper off.

When I was teaching I was quite happy, after decades of taking part in discussions that involved questions like, "Who was the unicorn last time?", to pass the responsibility of getting to the bottom of these profound issues to the younger generation. Apart from all the other benefits of peer mediation, nine- and ten-year-olds can empathize with the world of make-believe in a much more immediate and genuine way; and when disputes arise with the youngest children, it is vital that a mediator appreciate how real and serious it is to the children involved. Even when it has to do with imaginary light sabres. And you can't smile!

DEMOCRACY IN ACTION

> *"I love our teachers because whenever something comes up, they don't just talk to each other about it, they bring it up at Meeting. Then the whole school gets a say. Meetings are excellent because you can say what you think and the teachers take everything seriously."*
> — Sophie Brauer, Grade 7 student (Halifax Independent School alumna)

If one of the goals of education is to raise children who will contribute to a healthy society, children need to be exposed to what that means from an early age. It is important that children experience the empowerment that happens when they feel they have an influence over decisions that affect their lives.

Whole-school Meetings, where students discuss items of importance to them, are one way in which Halifax Independent School students can experience real democracy. These are not the assemblies I experienced in Britain, where the whole school would sit quietly while an authority figure would present news, rules, lectures about behaviour or introduce performances. Having a truly participatory Meeting with the three-hundred-plus pupils of most modern schools is difficult, which is why many schools have assemblies rather than meetings.

Meeting

Agenda
1. Indoor Shoes — Jake
2. Name Calling — Josy
3. Four Square — Terry, Peter and Jamila

1. Teacher: "Jake, what do you have to say about Indoor Shoes?"
   Jake: "Well, today, when I came in from snack, there was mud all over the circle area. I sat down in it, and my pants got all dirty."
   Teacher: "Hmm, that's not very pleasant. What can we do about it?"
   Jake: "Well, people aren't supposed to wear their indoor shoes outside. I think that's what happened. The playground was really muddy today."
   Teacher: "So, you want to remind everyone about the rule about shoes?"
   Jake: "Yes, indoor shoes for indoors only!"
   Teacher: "Thanks for reminding us, Jake."
2. Josy: "Today at snack time, someone called me 'Red.'"
   Teacher: "And how did you feel about that?"
   Josy: "I felt bad. I don't like it when people make fun of my hair."
   Teacher: "Does anyone have a comment to make about this situation? James?"
   James: "I've heard lots of people calling Josy 'Red.'"
   Josy: "I only like it when my friends call me that. So I know they are not making fun of me."
   Teacher: "If someone hears people calling you that, how do they know they shouldn't?"
   Josy: "Because they are not my friend."
   Teacher: "Can anyone tell me if we have a rule about this situation?"
   Saul: "You shouldn't call anyone by a name that is not their own."
   Teacher: "And why is that?"

> Saul: "Because it's hard to tell if someone is making fun of you. So it's better if you just call people by their own names."
> Teacher: "Does that make sense, Josy?"
> Josy: "I guess so."
> Teacher: "Does anyone else have anything to add?"
> James: "I think people who have nicknames shouldn't use them at school unless they want everyone to call them that. How are you supposed to know if you are a friend or not?"
> Teacher: "That's a good suggestion."
> 3. Terry: "Well, when we are playing four square, it seems that the Elders (Grade 5 and 6 students) keep changing the rules, so that they never get out."
> Teacher: "Do you mean all the Elders?"
> Terry: "No, I guess not, only some of them."
> Teacher: "Okay then, I can see that you are upset about this. Can you give me an example?"
>
> A long discussion about the ever-changing rules of four square follows, resulting in the meeting going into overtime. The children are very engaged, and passionate about the perceived unfairness, so the teacher asks for some volunteers to get together to decide on some rules for four square that can be adopted by everyone. The teacher also agrees to help, and the group set up a time at lunchtime to meet. They consult the Internet for "official rules," but draw up a set of rules that is adapted to the Halifax Independent School situation. The following week, the rules are posted and adopted by the whole school.

"Meetings" already had a long tradition at Halifax Independent School when I started there, and have always been important in its life. Let's take a look at how this one aspect of school helps students learn to contribute to a healthy democracy, and thereby helps to shape a sense of community.

Kids at Meeting.

Other than the no name-calling rule, most rules at Halifax Independent School were set over the years by the students themselves at Meetings. Students set the agenda, and although there are sometimes announcements by teachers, most of the items are contributed by the children and reflect their concerns.

The focus of the Meetings is on problem solving, but the gatherings are also a wonderful experience of democracy in action. Problems that are brought up must be of interest to a wider group than just one class, and often result in changes to school rules. When it seemed that every second meeting was dealing with problems with snow fort building (and destroying) on the playground, the children were asked how to solve the problems. Different suggestions were put forth, but all involved establishing a new rule. One suggested rule was, "you should never destroy anyone's snow fort." Another was, "you should only destroy the snow fort that you helped build." The students voted on which rule to accept, and the second won — probably in recognition of the fun you can have in building a structure, and then tearing it down and starting over. The sense of empowerment that a child feels after being part of solving a problem with the whole school, or having input into a rule change that affects everyone, is good preparation for later participation in civil society.

There are some basic rules for Meetings that are strictly adhered to. One of them is that names should never be used when discussing a problem — if a person is to be referred to, she should be referred to as "someone." This avoids embarrassing or putting children on the defensive. What can often happen in this situation is that the "someone" involved (perhaps James in the example above) will make a comment to present another side of the story. Another rule is that issues should only be brought up at Meeting if other ways of solving the problem have been tried and failed. In the name-calling example, Josy may have been asked to bring the problem up at Meeting because the teachers noticed an increase in name-calling and felt that the children needed a reminder of the rule, and also an exploration of why that rule is in place. Finally, respect for all is a fundamental rule that involves listening to the person who is speaking, not interrupting and not laughing when a small child brings up something that seems silly or boring to the older children.

Again, all this takes time. But by giving children input into creating the rules that govern life on the playground, and decision-making power over things that affect their daily lives, we are not only increasing their buy-in (making it more likely they will follow the rules), but we are creating a community. Being part of a democratic community is good preparation for eventually contributing to a healthy society.

COOPERATION

Many school systems stress competition — in a very simplistic, individualized sense. The competition that used to be about getting into the best universities has filtered down to the elementary level, and even preschool in some countries. In the video introducing the US's Common Core curriculum,[87] the narrator tells us, "Life is full of measuring sticks . . . how smart we are, how fast we are, how well we can, you know, compete. But up until now it's been pretty hard to know how well kids are competing in school, and how well they're gonna do when they get out of school." The message is that school and life itself is the endless competition of individuals. It comes from the very top levels of government, and is reinforced through the testing that children experience in school.

Of course, the world is sometimes a competitive place, and competitiveness is a human trait like any other. But very often, individuals have to cooperate in groups in order to compete effectively as teams. Percy Buffington's research shows that cooperation is at least as important for survival as competition.[88] Even in highly competitive team sports, cooperation is essential for success. The star shooter on a basketball team can't accomplish much if no one passes her the ball. So, how do we expect children to learn about cooperation? If the hidden curriculum is teaching one thing (competition), it will be difficult to counteract it, no matter how many programs we implement.

The ability to work cooperatively with others is a social skill that is becoming more acknowledged in the

Cooperation.

working world. This can be taught explicitly. But even more important is the hidden curriculum: the way the teachers, administrators and parents work together, and the horizontal teaching style practised by teachers.

Children learn by example — if you want children to cooperate, it helps if they see adults around them cooperating. In a small school like Halifax Independent, there are many opportunities for the adults to demonstrate cooperation. The children see parents and teachers meeting together to make important decisions about the school. Work parties in which children, parents and teachers come together to fix something or to do a spring cleanup are an excellent example of cooperation in action, and contribute to a sense of community that the children will long remember. Children also see teachers working together, consulting each other on issues, planning together and socializing together. In short, a school that demonstrates a high degree of "social capital" (an economic term defined by the OECD as "networks together with shared norms, values and understandings that facilitate cooperation within or among groups")[89] is more likely to encourage cooperative behaviour among students.

The ability to work cooperatively is a skill that needs to be taught — both in practice through working in groups, through the "horizontal" teaching style and from the collaborative climate of the school community itself.

MULTI-AGE CLASSES: EXTENDING THE FAMILY INTO THE SCHOOL

One of the many ways in which the world of today's children differs from the world of the last century is that for much of the latter, most children grew up in large families and often in crowded neighbourhoods. In that context, children learned from their older siblings — and those eldest helped with the younger ones. Today's families tend to be much smaller and more isolated from nearby communities.

Children learn a great deal from each other in the socio-emotional realm. In the conflict mediation example, older children are helping younger children. They are role models, modelling cooperation, generosity and concentration. It is great for the younger children, but also wonderful for the older ones, who get a chance to be helpful, kind, wise and looked up to. This is why it has never made sense to me that our school system slots children into groups where everyone is the same age.

At Halifax Independent School, almost all classes are "multi-age" classrooms. In multi-age classes, children are placed in groups that encompass more than one grade or age level, and this requires a completely different teaching approach. In multi-age classes, which can be two or more age levels with one teacher, teachers teach one basic curriculum, with many adaptations for the differing developmental levels in the class. These are different from "split classes," where two grades are taught by one teacher but each grade curriculum is taught largely independently.

Multi-age classes at Halifax Independent School allow the teachers to teach individuals rather than grades. They are able to account for each child's needs, abilities in different areas, developmental levels and learning styles. They lend themselves perfectly to any kind of inquiry or theme teaching; academic learning does not suffer when children learn with younger or older children.

Children who work with classmates of different ages will have the opportunity to observe others doing easier and more difficult work, and to form a clear idea of what they are working toward. They are able to evaluate their own work more realistically, and often find it motivating to have examples of work that they can aspire to. The expectation is that all children will do their best work. This does not mean that they are all expected to perform at the same level, but they know that if they maintain their best effort, they will one day master what seems difficult today.

Teachers in multi-age classrooms must pay great attention to children's rates of development. In a given class of six- and seven-year-olds, you may find a group of children reading chapter books, another group that is happy with picture books, another sounding out simple, predictable books and still another group that is working on learning their letter sounds. This range of literacy development levels could easily be found in a single grade class.

Progressive, horizontal teaching lends itself perfectly to multi-age groupings. The intrinsically interesting topics and the initial brainstorms that help set the direction for study are accessible to all children regardless of age. Reading material can be chosen to meet the reading levels of the children in the class, but many resources — films, guest speakers, experiments or games — can be used with the whole class. All the children benefit from the discussion afterward, in which different perspectives are explored and points are clarified for children who may not have understood or who may have missed a crucial part. The teacher will vary the expectations for work to be done depending on the child, being careful to set them at a level that will be challenging but not discouraging.

But the major benefit of multi-age classes is the potential for socio-emotional learning and the development of a solid sense of community. It is not for nothing that multi-age classes are sometimes referred to as "family" groupings.

In multi-age classes, children get to know well children not only of their own age group, but also those older and younger. They will experience being part of the younger group, but in a year or two they will be in the oldest group in their class and as such have the chance to be leaders. Older children solidify their knowledge and skills by helping younger students.

In these classes, teachers generally teach the same children (although perhaps in different configurations) for more than one year, allowing them to deepen their bonds with the children and monitor progress over a longer term; this works well with the need to know each child in order to differentiate the learning experiences presented. The nurturing and supportive environment that is encouraged in multi-age classes ensures that children experience little anxiety over their progress. Pass-or-fail grading does not happen — children stay with their age group throughout elementary school.

Multi-age classrooms, once fairly common in school systems in the English-speaking world and beyond, are falling victim to the emphasis on standards-based education. When children are tested at every grade level, as they are now in many states in the US with the new Common Core curriculum, or when grade-level outcomes are very specific, as they are in many Canadian schools, teachers must teach to those standards — a task that becomes more difficult with more grade levels. This is a pity, because as Pardini outlines in her 2005 article, "The Slowdown of Multi-age Classrooms,"[90] "Students in multi-age settings were found to have higher self-esteem, more positive self-concepts, less anti-social behaviour and better attitudes toward school than their peers in single-grade classes." This has been my experience with multi-age teaching. I would add that it is easier to teach cooperation, critical thinking skills, leadership and empathy in multi-age groups when there are older children who lead the way.

NEIGHBOURHOOD SCHOOLS AND SCHOOL SIZE

The last fifty years have seen a huge shift in Canada to larger, consolidated schools. Most people of my generation went to elementary schools in their neighbourhood, with under two hundred students. Since then, rural consolidation has meant fewer, larger schools, longer bus rides, and many rural communities becoming bedroom communities to the larger towns with the schools. In cities, schools have grown too, and school boundaries have become a contentious issue, especially when some schools are deemed better than others.

Changing demographics within cities mean that some neighbourhood schools are losing students while others are bursting at the seams.

The smaller, neighbourhood school where teachers know whole families of children (and may even have taught their parents), and where children can play after-hours with their neighbourhood friends from school has a lot of attraction for many parents. In these days of more mobility, smaller families and stressful jobs, the school can be an oasis of stability for children (and their parents). Neighbourhood schools can also be a focal point for community activity, and can attract businesses and families to locate to their area. With autonomy over curriculum, these schools can develop socially responsible curricula rooted in their particular community, using local issues as a springboard, and steeping children in their history and culture.

Small schools, like Halifax Independent School, which has under two hundred children, tend to do well with the social side of learning. Seeing children in the context of their family and community gives teachers insight into their personalities. Even though Halifax Independent's students come from all parts of the city and beyond, it has become a community in itself, with strong ties between families and teachers.

The same studies pointing to a stronger sense of belonging and greater participation in extracurricular activities for students in small schools also show that there is more interaction between teachers and students.[91] In addition, small schools show greater teacher satisfaction and cooperation — all good indicators of higher social capital and predictors of a positive school climate.

Unfortunately, keeping local schools open, whether rural or urban, is not often a priority for school boards. They claim that it is not an economically sound practice when enrolment falls below a certain level. But by closing these schools, they are doing a double disservice to the community — taking away the heart of a community, as well as the opportunity for children to benefit from the family atmosphere of a smaller school.

I had the experience of advocating, with other parents, to keep my daughter's small, rural school open. During this time, I was repeatedly assured of the benefits of "economies of scale" — that my child would benefit from the many more resources that would be possible by combining several small schools into one. These claims can be highly suspect. Board savings by closing schools are not as great as they often claim, "if and when you factor-in the operating costs per square foot, the actual cost per graduate, the added cost of bussing students, and the often inflated costs of new school construction."[92] I would add that since the biggest single expense in education is teacher salaries, and if school boards are committed to keeping class size at similar levels across their districts, the "savings" of school closures would be minimal.

Closing schools is guaranteed to galvanize parents, and the more powerful the parent lobby, the less likely they are to close. At the same time, rural schools may lack those powerful voices and are more vulnerable. Underlying most school reviews is the assumption by education bureaucrats that school size has no bearing on academic achievement. In recent years, there has been more research about the optimal size of schools. One study finds that larger schools have a significant negative effect on math and reading achievement, and that this is particularly strong in Grades 6 to 10.[93] The average Finnish school (156 students) is less than half the size of the average Canadian school, and this reflects a deliberate policy choice.[94]

One barrier to keeping smaller, local schools open is the attitude toward "split classes" — that they should be avoided at all costs. If we think of them as multi-age classes instead, they become a positive choice and allow more flexibility when it comes to keeping class sizes reasonable. They can be a way of ensuring that small schools remain viable. It allows small schools to enrich their social groups based on interests and personalities rather than age alone.

Everyone suffers when small, local schools close — students, parents and the community. But the teachers also suffer, especially if they have fought and lost the battle to keep their school open. It's a double blow for them — they have not been listened to and their working conditions have been altered, often for the worse.

Nova Scotia Small Schools Initiative
In Nova Scotia, recent cutbacks in education, combined with declining enrolments, especially in rural areas, led to a series of school reviews that recommended the closure of several small, rural schools. Around the same time, a report commissioned by the government, the Ivany Report, was advocating rural revitalization and stated, "Schools, in particular rural schools, can play an important part in the development of business and entrepreneurial activity in Nova Scotia." Parent and community groups rallied together and managed to pressure the government into putting a stop to school closures until a fairer process could be developed. A new review process, in which boards are required to engage in long-range planning with all stakeholders, was finally completed in 2014.

> The Nova Scotia Small Schools Initiative was started by a group of parents and other interested citizens with the goal of placing "our community schools at the heart of a well coordinated Rural Strategy." One of the cofounders, Kate Oland, said, "I'm pretty tired of being characterized as hysterical, emotional, nostalgic and backwards" when she talks about the value schools have to their communities.
>
> The NSSSI tries to establish a business case for keeping small schools open: what business interest will be able to attract workers to a community in which their children will have to be bussed to school for hours each day? They set about helping each community develop plans for what educator Dr. David Clandfield called "community hub schools," in which communities work together to find new, creative ways of addressing underutilized space. Clandfield cites the example of Toronto closing small schools, and then selling them to private interests that establish new and thriving schools in the same buildings. The implication is that if private interests can make these buildings profitable, why can't there be a partnership between small schools and other groups (either not-for-profit or private)?

BUILDING A CLIMATE FROM THE BOTTOM UP

Schools are mini-societies. Children learn so much more in them than academic subjects, but socio-emotional learning does not have to be at the expense of academics — it can go hand in hand with it, and indeed will enhance it.

Halifax Independent School has been in the fortunate position of having been set up to focus on the whole child, and the socio-emotional realm has always been important. Over its forty plus years, it has had to reinvent itself many times, and each time was an opportunity to reevaluate and enhance its climate. Often, the hidden curriculum would be examined to make sure that it was still aligned with what the school is explicitly teaching. Was the assessment system still focused on helping students learn and encouraging a growth mindset? Did the community give each member a chance to contribute? Were children still learning about solving social problems by actually practising conflict resolution themselves?

Dedicated to raising children who will "make the world a little less cruel and heartless," Halifax Independent has consciously and explicitly identified and taught collaborative values and social skills. This is important work and has been so much more effective because it has built its positive school climate from the bottom up.[95]

Chapter 7
MEASURING UP: AUTHENTIC ASSESSMENT

> *"Each box that you mark on each test that you take,*
> *Remember your teachers, their jobs are at stake,*
> *Your score is their score, but don't get too stressed,*
> *They'd never teach anything, not on the test."*
> — Tom Chapin, "Not on the Test"

Teachers in public schools are spending ever increasing amounts of their time assessing children, whether it is marking class tests, filling in report cards or administering standardized exams. In Britain, it is estimated that up to 20 per cent of class time is devoted to some kind of assessment.[96] What is the purpose of all this? Is it actually helping children learn?

> **Report Card Day**
> "Time to do our report cards!" announces the teacher to her class of eight- and nine-year-olds. "Let's brainstorm some categories that we can use." The children start calling out various subject areas such as "writing," "drawing," "research," "math," as the teacher writes them on the board. She probes a little further, and elicits some categories in the social area such as "solving conflicts" and

> "responsibility." She then suggests adding an "effort" line for each subject area. Passing out lined paper, the teacher asks the children to design their own "report card," and use their own rating system to assess themselves. She asks if anyone knows why they are doing this, and generates a lively discussion about the benefits of self-assessment. Then she reminds them to think about their own progress since the beginning of the year, not about anyone else's. The children eagerly settle down to work, as the teacher circulates, talking with each child about some of their responses.
>
> When the buzz has died down and the teacher collects the "report cards," she is struck by the individuality of each one. Some have borrowed the traditional report card format and given themselves As, Bs and Cs. Other responses range from happy/neutral/sad faces to elaborate colour-coded keys. But the truly amazing thing is how close to the teacher's opinion they generally are — and in the rare cases where there is a big difference, it is cause for useful investigation. For example, when Erin, a generally happy-go-lucky child, gave herself an FFF for "being a good friend," the teacher queried it, and heard all about Erin's difficulties fitting in with a group of girls that she wanted to play with.
>
> This type of self-assessment is a great starting point for conversations with parents at parent-teacher interviews, but, more importantly, it helps the children identify areas where they need more work and to reflect on what they are really good at. It actually helps children learn, which should be the main goal for any kind of assessment system.

When I was growing up, I believed that IQ tests had an almost mystical power. After all, in Grade 7, we were streamed into no less than eight classes, each of which supposedly contained students with differing levels of intellectual ability, all based on the IQ tests we had taken in

Music	I think I have been doing pretty well in Music
French	I like French, but I'm not 100% shure that I'm doing good.
Art	I'm 89% shure I'm doing good in Art.
Phys. Ed.	I love Phys. Ed. and I think I'm doing good in it.
Theme	I am 100% shure I'm doing great in theam.
Math	I am 99% shure I am doing good in Math.
Reading	I think I'm doing great in Reading.
Writing	I think I'm doing good in Writing.

Olds self-evaluation.

Grade 6. In high school we were lumped into academic, technical and vocational classes, and our future depended on which stream we were in. It's no wonder that I attributed such power to the IQ tests that seemed to have so much effect on people's lives.

When I encountered real tests and exams for the first time in high school, I found that I was pretty good at them, especially the multiple choice ones (using a certain amount of strategic guessing). I did well on the scholastic achievement tests at the end of high school and got into a good university. But I don't remember many occasions in high school where I was excited by a project or put anything other than minimal effort into any of my assignments. I didn't have to — I got good marks because I could always "cram" for the final exam. I thought I was pretty smart, and most people around me seemed to agree with me. We were all victims of the "fixed mindset," and testing just reinforced this.

It wasn't until I was at university that I started to question the purpose of this whole assessment system. During my first semester, I got a shock. To get through my courses, it wasn't enough to skim and regurgitate. The professors expected us to understand the material deeply, and make intelligent observations. We needed to analyze and dissect theories, and the math courses demanded that we figure out abstract concepts on our own. I didn't do so well on the first midterms. Was it possible the SATs were all wrong, and I wasn't as smart as I thought I was? Doubt set in. I soon realized that I needed to work hard throughout the term, and that cramming for the exams was not enough.

Then I took a course in "psychometrics," otherwise known as psychological measurement, which taught us about the design, marking and interpretation of IQ and other psychological tests. It also taught me about the inherent fallibility of standardized tests, including achievement tests — specifically, the cultural, class and intellectual bias built into them. I was dismayed at the thought of how many students were shut out of educational opportunities because of these very imperfect tests.

It was when I started my first teaching job that I began to seriously question the role that testing played in education. My first students were non-English-speaking Cree and Inuit children, so I was fairly quickly doused with some cold realities. I found out that my students didn't enjoy tests the way I had — a small proportion might, but a much larger group found them extremely stressful and anxiety producing. If they didn't do well (according to their own standards), the tests would be devastating to their self-esteem. I knew there must be a better way of assessing children.

Later on, teaching in a secondary school in Nigeria, I saw the realities of a strictly exam-based curriculum. At the time,

Nigeria was following the Cambridge curriculum, complete with final school-exit exams, all commissioned in Britain. There was no attempt to make them culturally appropriate and no allowances were made for the fact that most students were exposed to English for the first time in secondary school. Our teaching was completely bound by the syllabus, and I got a strong lesson in "teaching to the test." Many times, while teaching English literature, I would just feel like I was making a breakthrough with the students and actually generating some real discussion, when a voice from the back of the class would yell, "Syllabus, syllabus!" We would have to resume our narrow quest for the right answers to sample test questions. My teaching seemed very futile when only about 2 per cent of our students were destined to pass the exams. For those that passed, the rewards were very high indeed (entrance to university, international scholarships). But for the vast majority who failed, the system not only did not help them learn the material, it actually deprived most of them of opportunities for real learning.

But it was when I worked in an English junior school in Colchester, UK, that I really appreciated how deeply a school system that puts standardized testing at its centre can actually impede true student learning.

Frequent standardized testing in Britain, coupled with a rigorous school inspection process and the publication of results in annual "league tables," has created a huge infrastructure of assessing children, teachers and schools — and helping students learn seemed to me to be low on the agenda.

Part of my job in Colchester was to give literacy support to a small group of twelve eight-year-olds who had failed the literacy portion of the first standardized test children take at age seven. Four of them had severe learning problems, but the rest were normal, bright eight-year-olds who had just taken a little longer than average to learn to read. Nevertheless, all these children were referred to by staff as the "LA" children — that is, "Least Able." Already labeled "losers" at the age of seven and smart enough to know it, they showed us every day, with their anxiety, anger and acting out, that they deeply resented their assigned status.

Much of what I was expected to do with these children was to get them ready for the next round of standardized curriculum tests. The four with severe learning problems had no hope of passing these tests, and the rest were bored and frustrated by the constant test practise. As the head teacher explained to me, "It is stressful to everyone, because we all suffer if the school doesn't improve on last year's results." Schools would be considered to be "cheating" if they did not test their lowest performing students, or if teachers helped them by doing such things as reading the instructions, or sounding out the odd word that students couldn't decipher. The children I taught were not helped by the streaming that can be a result of this kind of testing, and as PISA shows, does not actually raise the general level of academic achievement.

I witnessed firsthand the chilling effects that standardized tests in Britain have on education. One of the most obvious dimensions is teaching to the test, and I saw the low morale among the teachers at my school who were afraid to teach anything not on the curriculum. There was also a narrowing of the curriculum — the arts, socio-emotional learning and horizontal teaching all suffer when the focus has to be preparing children for all the tests.

Apathy and disengagement of students who do less well on the tests is another major cost. High drop-out rates

(18 per cent of twenty-five- to thirty-four-year-olds in the UK have not finished upper secondary school)[97] and high truancy rates attest to the alienation from education that many British students feel. And many students (and teachers) are prone to the test anxiety that happens when so much is riding on the results of those tests.

After years of steadily losing my faith in most types of tests, I was lucky to land at Halifax Independent School. Unlike the many teachers I encountered who knew about the effects of standardized testing on children but felt powerless to change it, I was able to work in a school where the goal of assessment was to help the students learn, and at the same time let their parents know what is going on.

AUTHENTIC ASSESSMENT AT HALIFAX INDEPENDENT SCHOOL

A standardized test may be able to provide a measure of what a child did achieve on a particular day, but measuring what a child did do does not reveal what the child could do. If the objective of assessment is to help individual children develop to their full potential, teacher assessments of what each child could achieve are essential. Authentic assessment "aims to evaluate students' abilities in 'real-world' contexts."[98] It compares children with themselves.

At Halifax Independent, in the elementary years, formal testing is not part of the culture. When tests are introduced, it is done in a gradual and non-threatening way. But this does not mean that children are not very carefully monitored and assessed. In fact, one of the school's promises — "we know your child" — indicates that assessment is taken very seriously. However, authentic assessment does not involve merely ticking boxes, marking tests and generating computer comments. There are no report cards until middle school (Grades 7 to 9); the goal of assessment is to encourage children to take responsibility for their own learning and to keep parents informed about their progress.

Some of the methods Halifax Independent School uses to assess children include:

- Constant verbal feedback to children as they are working, and written and verbal feedback on completed assignments.

- Portfolio assessment: when a child joins the school, a large folder is created for them, and every term, a few representative samples of their original writing, theme work, math and artwork are added to it. These samples are dated, and accumulate over the years into a full record of the child's progress. Portfolios are often used to monitor a child's development and progress from year to year, and at the end of the school stay, they are given back as a memento/record of development.

- Benchmarks: over the years, benchmarks for each level have been developed that cover the skill areas in theme, mathematics and other specialist subjects children are expected to master at each level. Categories for each skill to be checked off are, generally: "exposure", "at level" and "ready to move on", with space for a comment. These benchmarks are filled in three times a year, just before parent-teacher interviews. They are used to help teachers present a realistic and detailed picture of each child to the parents, as well as to plan ways to either extend or reinforce skills. The benchmarks were originally developed using the Nova Scotia public school curriculum as a baseline, but have been modified and extended over the years.

- Extensive notes: teachers conduct frequent informal assessments and keep notes on their results. Before parent-teacher interviews, these notes are compiled and, along with the benchmarks, are used as the basis for the interviews. Highlights from the benchmarks (strengths and weaknesses), work habits, social development and anecdotes about events within the classroom let parents know that their child is known and appreciated. Notes and benchmarks are kept in the child's file. They are not generally shown to the parents unless there is a specific request made.

- Teacher meetings: before parent-teacher interviews, time is set aside for teachers to meet in small groups to discuss every student they are involved with, and notes from these meetings are used in the interviews. Often these meetings reveal patterns of behaviour, difficulties or even a burgeoning talent that might not have seemed important before.

- Parent contact: there are three formal parent-teacher interviews throughout the year, but there are many other opportunities for contact between parents and teachers (daily pickups and drop-offs, school social events, volunteering within the classroom). Social and emotional progress is reported on in addition to academics. Regular phone calls home are invaluable for hearing about any concerns parents may have, or passing on positive information. Classroom websites, curriculum meetings and regular notes home keep parents informed about activities within the classroom as well as special events. Any more serious concerns on the part of either the teacher or the parent can be dealt with at an after-school meeting.

- Fairs: the twice-yearly Fairs are an ideal opportunity for parents to see how their children are doing in the context of their peer group. The speeches, which are written, memorized and delivered by each child, give an insight into their writing skills, depth of understanding of the topic, confidence and presentation skills. The informal question and answer sessions afterward allow each child to be an expert, and the displays show off their best work. Displays are carefully designed to feature every child equally, and become a goal for them to work towards.

- Quizzes and tests: biweekly, individualized spelling quizzes or other forms of spelling assessment are often given to children at the upper elementary level. Math tests, often individualized and based on the benchmarks, are introduced to nine-year-olds and given more formally to ten- and eleven-year-olds. Much time is spent with the children analyzing their own test results, and it is emphasized that the marks are mainly to help teachers and children identify where more work is needed. Since the marks do not contribute to an overall grade, are not broadcast publicly and children are given the opportunity to correct any mistakes, anxiety and the possible adverse impact on their self-esteem is minimized.

- Self-assessment: from the age of six, children are encouraged to evaluate their own work realistically. One of the ways this happens is that once or twice a year, they create a self-assessment tool or "report card," and fill it in themselves.

- Middle school: When children get to middle school, testing is one part of the overall evaluation. Since the majority of the students enter high schools where testing is a large part of the curriculum, these tests are seen as essential preparation for the "real world." Direct written and verbal feedback is given on all assignments and larger projects are graded. Rubrics are used frequently to allow students to assess themselves. All students are expected to work to the best of their ability, and work that is not satisfactory is redone until it meets the required standard. There is at least one Fair each year, where students present what they have learned, and occasional "open classes" where parents are invited in. Parent-teacher interviews are held three times per year and involve the entire team of teachers who give a rounded report of students' progress. Two report cards are sent home each year: in Grade 7 these are strictly anecdotal, whereas for the Grades 8 and 9, letter grades are given.

Many hours of teacher collaboration and research over the years means that these assessment procedures are constantly evolving. Many of the measures were not in place when I started at the school. The benchmarks were developed over several years, and are constantly updated to ensure that they change with the curriculum. The organization and use of portfolios was given a boost when a student teacher shared with the staff the latest theory on portfolio assessment, learned in her education program.

The collaboration of teachers is key to the development of well-rounded, authentic student assessment and the creation of meaningful measures of improvement.

> **Developing a writing assessment**
>
> Although Halifax Independent School only goes to Grade 9, we continued to hear news from our graduates for years. Their feedback and that from their parents reassured us that our graduates did exceedingly well in high school and beyond. However, in 2011, Halifax Independent School teachers decided that it would also be useful to have a writing assessment tool for the elementary level that would inform their teaching (and reassure them that their teaching of writing was on track).
>
> Over several days, teachers developed writing tasks and a rubric to use in evaluating them. With graded writing samples from other jurisdictions, the levels were calibrated to give an idea of where on the writing continuum students were. Ideas, Organization, Voice, Word Choice, Sentence Fluency, Punctuation and Spelling were all rated anonymously on a scale from one to six by at least two teachers, thus ensuring a measure of objectivity.
>
> When reporting to the students and their parents, the emphasis is always on what the children do well, the progress made since the last assessment and what they need to work on next. Because doing the assessment is time consuming, it is done sparingly. However, the process of developing the rubric was extremely valuable for the teachers, and is an example of the type of collaboration that enriches education. Why reinvent the wheel when there are many existing writing rubrics that could easily have been adopted? The answer is that the process of developing our own rubric allowed us an in-depth

> refresher of teaching writing that might not have otherwise happened. We had some interesting discussions, which cleared up some misconceptions and allowed us to create some shared definitions. For example, we discovered that some of us (including myself) weren't entirely clear how to assess a student's "voice." As a bonus, we also gained a tool that let us know if there were aspects of writing that we needed to focus on more with the children.

Also necessary for authentic assessment to work is a climate of acceptance, where students are able to accept constructive feedback and not feel shame in admitting when they are struggling with something. Some of the traditional methods of assessment actively work against creating this climate — some (standardized tests) are unfair or unreliable, and others (marks or grades) are just ineffective.

THE COSTS OF STANDARDIZED ASSESSMENT

Not only are the traditional methods of assessment ineffective at helping children learn, they also have very steep costs. Many of us have been brought up with the cultural imagery of struggling students who work hard to overcome adversity, and end up at the top of the class or winning a medal or gaining admittance to an exclusive school. GERM's emphasis on ranking glorifies the winners — however, only one child comes top of the class, and the other twenty-nine "lose." The cost of motivating the few is the demotivation of the many.

High- and low-stakes tests

A crucial distinction in testing is that between high-stakes and low-stakes testing. High-stakes tests are those whose scores have serious consequences for educators, students or schools. If test scores are used for "streaming" children into various programs or if students' career prospects depend on them, they are referred to as high-stakes tests. When teachers' pay or jobs depend on test results, or if schools are at risk of closing because of bad test scores, they are high stakes, and it stands to reason that their influence on the whole educational system is profound. GERM relies increasingly on standardized testing to monitor teachers and schools and mandate "improvement." High-stakes tests enable top-down control by central administrators over the entire education system — often justified using terms such as "accountability," "efficiency" or "raising standards." Their primary purpose is to compare students, teachers, schools and districts in order to allocate resources — the scholastic achievement tests in Britain are extremely high stakes. But it is questionable how much they help students learn.

High stakes testing also produces increased anxiety in students, falling morale for teachers and sometimes the loss of neighbourhood schools deemed "failing." Even when schools are not "punished" for poor test results, making the test results of individual schools public can set up a negative spiral for a school if one year's test scores cause the parents of "better" students to switch to other schools.

By contrast, the purpose of low-stakes tests is to assist learning by providing information to administrators, to teachers and to the takers of the test. In most low-stakes tests, the main comparison that is made is between an individual's or program's progress over time. For example, a teacher who administers a Diagnostic Reading Assessment to an individual child is looking to assess their strengths, their progress since the last assessment and their needs, as well as getting an idea of what level of book they can read. Tests that are administered to a representative sample of the population to assess how a program or teaching approach is working can be valuable to educational planning and curriculum development, but they are low stakes because they do not affect funding for individual schools.

Low-stakes standardized tests can help us understand better the process of education and can help students learn — either directly, by giving feedback on individual progress, or indirectly by improving programs or teaching methodologies. In this book I repeatedly use the results of such tests to show, for example, why Finland has better educational outcomes than the UK or the US. Such tests can also show, for example, the importance of music education or the impact of the age of learning to read.

> The PISA tests provide an illustration of the dangers of publicizing standardized test results. When PISA testing started out, they were a low-stakes test that made some very interesting connections between educational policies in different parts of the world and academic achievement. Over the years, however, as the media in various countries has started paying attention to them, they have become more and more high stakes, to the point where governments are overtly trying to boost their scores. The reaction to Canada's slipping math scores that came out in December 2013 (described in Chapter 3) is one example. It is clear that the development of the Common Core curriculum in the US and the new National Curriculum in Britain are at least partly a result of their countries' relatively poor showing on PISA — but both initiatives continue the vicious cycle of stressful testing and overall student underperformance.

A time for discussion.

In Canada, assessment has been more teacher driven than in many GERM countries, at least until recent years. Education is a provincial responsibility and report cards are often drawn up by local school boards. A low-stakes national testing program, the Pan-Canadian Assessment Program, assesses the achievement of thirteen-year-olds based on a representative sample of forty thousand students every three years. Individual results are not given or recorded, but the comparisons of regions or provinces definitely influence decision-making.

However, the influence of GERM can be felt here as well. All Canadian provinces now also give provincially designed standardized tests to children usually three or four times during their school careers, and most of them have provincially administered final exams for graduation.

Ontario has increased its reliance on standardized assessment in recent years. Its provincial testing agency, the

Education Quality and Accountability Office (EQAO), administers tests in literacy and math skills to all children in Grades 3, 6 and 9, and then the Ontario Secondary School Literacy Test in Grade 10. All students have to pass the Grade 10 literacy test to graduate, so it is very high stakes. Test results for individual schools are available to anyone on the EQAO's website for all levels, "to contribute to public accountability and to the continuous improvement on the part of every student."[99]

The Fraser Institute in BC and the Atlantic Institute for Market Studies in the East issue report cards on their regions' schools, and it is easy to find rankings for most other provinces. The provincial standardized tests are becoming more high stakes each year.

How do these high-stakes tests help children learn? Often the feedback to the students comes too late to help them, as they are marked in a central location by teachers who do not know them. Their contribution to real learning is minimal. In addition, these tests are expensive to create and mark in dollar terms, as well as in the time needed to administer them.

At Halifax Independent, tests embody the competitive world that students need to get ready for, and although the school recognizes that its students will someday face them, it also recognizes that failure on them at too early an age does not necessarily inspire students to work even harder. Halifax Independent knows that many non-resilient children will be discouraged and their self-esteem undermined.

The myth of objectivity
As a parent, I can identify with parents' desires to have some sort of "objective" measurement of their children's

accomplishments. After all, many of us grew up in environments where tests and marks gave us part of our identity. When my first daughter was born, I was thrilled when she started racing through those "milestones of development" that we read about. She walked at ten months (two months before the "average" child), spoke in full sentences at an early age and read books before she was five. I was convinced she was a genius. Then she started school, and took a break from her hectic race to maturity. She became an "average" child (who has since become a highly successful adult), and that was quite fine.

One of the rationales for GERM's reliance on standardized tests is that they are considered an "objective" measure of how well children can read, write or do math. Teacher assessments, on the other hand, are denigrated as subjective, and possibly biased. In the low-trust world we live in, all kinds of motives have been ascribed to teachers: prejudice against certain individuals or groups, fear for their jobs if their class marks aren't high enough or lack of effort. Somehow, the makers of tests have escaped the same scrutiny.

No assessment method is perfect. Teacher assessments are subjective (which is not always a bad thing), but standardized tests, in spite of some governments' faith in their objectivity, can also be very misleading. There has been a great deal written about cultural and racial biases in standardized tests, but biases against students from lower socio-economic groups, students with disabilities or second-language learners are no less serious. When tests are high stakes, as they are in the US and Britain, this type of bias can have a drastic effect on equity within the school system, and exacerbate existing inequalities.

The achievement tests given in schools, particularly

multiple-choice tests, tend to measure only a subset of the multiple intelligences or learning styles. They can also actively discriminate against certain types of intelligence. Peter, a boy I taught in Britain, was marked wrong on a reading comprehension test for answering the question, "Why did he buy the tiniest bun in the shop?" with "Because he wasn't hungry." The answer was supposed to be, "Because he didn't have enough money." Peter's response was a perfectly reasonable answer — just not what the examiner expected. Answers like these could have had a huge impact on the course of his life if the question had been on a high-stakes test that decided what secondary school he would be eligible to attend. Often, higher order thinking skills, critical thinking and creativity are simply not measured on achievement tests.

In this imperfect world, true objectivity in assessment is impossible to achieve. The human cost of chasing this myth is teachers who lose confidence in the value of their feedback, and students who are discriminated against and are shut out of opportunities because of their backgrounds or learning styles.

Report cards
Too often, schools have to use report cards and other assessment tools that have been created at a higher bureaucratic level. Some have an overwhelming number of categories and boxes to be ticked; others are anecdotal, in which teachers use computer generated comments to write a full paragraph about each student in each subject.

Most of the teachers I know who must use report cards dread that time of year. It is stressful and difficult to craft carefully worded paragraphs that must not paper over problems, but at the same time not offend the parents. It is stressful too for the principal or department head, who has to review all report cards — a grammar error or slightly inappropriate comment must not be allowed to slip by. It is no wonder administrators sometimes prefer formulaic comments.

Recently in Nova Scotia, there was an outcry from a significant number of parents about report cards and the "vague . . . boiler-plate" computer-generated language used in them.[100] A year later, the Department of Education directed teachers to include a personalized statement, without using jargon, which would include suggestions for parents on what they could do to support the child at home.

At least with the personalized statement, the parents could feel that there was a human being teaching their children. Real teacher autonomy, however, would allow schools and teachers to collaborate on the type of assessment that is appropriate to their unique situations, and decide on their own methods. This might include ditching report cards entirely in favour of more authentic assessment. After all, as one parent interviewed on CTV put it, "I don't pay as much attention to the report card as I do with my communications to the school and with the teachers, back and forth."[101] I suspect she speaks for many parents.

If teachers did not have to spend so many hours crafting report cards that met all the requirements, perhaps they would have more time to spend doing authentic assessment that could be reported directly in more intensive meetings with parents. I suspect that report cards are more to do with keeping parents happy than with really helping children take responsibility for their own learning, at least in the elementary years.

CAN AUTHENTIC ASSESSMENT WORK FOR ALL SCHOOLS?

Many people think that we need the marks from report cards and tests, standardized and otherwise, to motivate children to work hard. At Halifax Independent, I was often asked how we could possibly motivate children without them. The answer to that question lies in the integrated nature of the theme approach, or any approach in which curiosity and excitement about learning is built in and modelled by the teachers. Each child is expected to do their best work, and is held to a high standard, but it is a standard unique to each child. Small classes ensure that teachers get to know each child and their strengths well. Children are also encouraged to know their own limits and strengths, and to get satisfaction from knowing their work is the best they can do. This is intrinsic motivation, motivation that comes from inside a person, as opposed to extrinsic motivation, based on external rewards. A large volume of research shows that intrinsic motivation leads to increased creativity, and that reliance on extrinsic rewards can have the effect of killing creativity.[102] Since Halifax Independent School students generally don't experience the grading process until middle school, the highly creative work I have seen them do is not for the reward of marks.

At Halifax Independent School, it is not only the teachers that give honest feedback and constructive criticism; children are also taught how to give and receive feedback, and often peer acceptance is more motivating for children than any marks or grades would be. "Read Alouds," where children prepare and read a passage from a book they are enjoying, begin at an early age, and constructive feedback from the group is encouraged and modelled. It is not

Demonstrating an experiment at Fair.

uncommon to hear a seven-year-old comment, "I think you chose a good book, but you should have practised a bit more — there were a lot of difficult words." The skill of giving feedback that incorporates both a positive message and constructive criticism is one that is reinforced repeatedly and allows children to feel that they are a part of the learning that is going on around them. They are also encouraged to apply this assessment to themselves (apart from their yearly formal self-assessments) and a common question a teacher will ask when being shown a piece of work is "How do you feel about it?" I have observed over and over that children who are confident in their ability to give and receive feedback can enjoy the appreciation of their peers. Often it is all the motivation they need.

Authentic assessment as practised at Halifax Independent School, and the intrinsic motivation that is encouraged, much more closely reflects what happens in the real, outside-of-school world. Students who are not conditioned to work for marks on report cards or tests are more likely to become creative, collaborative participants in the working world. Schools that reduce the use of external rewards will find that this transition from extrinsic to intrinsic motivation will increase the level of creativity and participation. It doesn't happen immediately, but given the right conditions, it can happen anywhere. Finland is one of the few countries in the world that has recognized this.

Finland avoids mandatory standardized tests for all students at the pre-secondary level, but always comes close to the top of the PISA rankings. Pasi Sahlberg describes the assessment in Finland thus, "Although students are not tested in Finland as they are in many other countries, this does not mean that there is no assessment of students in Finland — quite the opposite." Their assessment is based mostly on teacher feedback — diagnostic, formative and summative assessment of the students by teachers. They use twice yearly report cards that are developed by the individual schools. Any national assessments that are done take place only every three to four years, and use sample-based methodology so that only 10 per cent of a given age group is tested. The only high-stakes tests within the Finnish education system are the National Matriculation Examinations, which are taken when students finish their secondary education at the age of eighteen or nineteen.[103] Finland shows us that what has worked so well at Halifax Independent, authentic assessment, can work in any school system that chooses to create the right conditions.

It has been a long road for me to wean myself off the idea that there is some uniform "objective" metre stick out there against which we can compare children. The more I learned about those measures, the more I was happy, as a parent, to just talk to my children's teachers for an honest assessment of how they were doing. As a teacher, I regained confidence in my judgment about children's progress and development, and was able to use truly authentic assessment in ways that really did help them learn.

Authentic assessment encourages real, in-depth learning, instead of the constant preparation and "cramming" for tests. Best of all, it promotes an atmosphere in which children and teachers have the confidence in themselves to take the risks that lead to real learning. It can happen anywhere.

Chapter 8
WHAT TEACHERS NEED: AUTONOMY, TRUST AND A CULTURE OF COLLABORATION

> *"There are two kinds of teachers: the kind that fill you with so much quail shot that you can't move, and the kind that just gives you a little prod behind and you jump to the skies."*
>
> — *Robert Frost*

If there is one thing that all sides in education debates agree on, it is that teachers matter. Endless studies have been published saying that excellent teachers are the key school factor to great outcomes in education.[104] Yet the discussion gets tricky when educators, administrators or economists try to define "excellence," and even more so when they suggest ways to promote it.

I have seen that when teachers love their jobs and are treated like professionals, it sets the stage for excellent, progressive teaching. Progressive teaching is more complex, more varied and more interesting than teaching to the test — in a real sense, it is harder work. It does not require extraordinary paragons to carry it out, but it does require a supportive school environment.

As we have seen, progressive teaching is predicated on the

Planting with a parent.

teacher's role as facilitator. The teacher is part of the inquiry process; he or she is a researcher in the fullest sense, both researching what works pedagogically, but also learning along with the children. A teacher's genuine enthusiasm for learning is infectious. Most of us remember boring teachers from our childhoods who droned on, expecting us to reproduce their words on the next test. It was not just the students that found this deadly — this kind of "vertical" teaching can also lead to staleness and boredom for the teachers doing it. Unfortunately many educational administrators believe that as long as a teacher knows the subject content, knows what students will be tested on and is capable of transferring this knowledge to the students in time for it to produce good test results, they are "excellent." In this view, transmitting a love of learning to students is not a priority.

When the teacher is a facilitator of the children's learning, the children do the learning; they are actively working on their education, not passively "being taught." As a teacher, I help them to learn how to learn, and in the process, experience the joy of making new connections, finding out interesting facts and reaching new levels of understanding. I participate fully in this process, experiencing all the highs and lows with the children. This type of teaching requires a lot of preparation — not just finding out all the information (which I could then just tell the children), but instead finding activities, experiences and materials that will engage, challenge and stimulate them in active learning. When it works well, it is deeply rewarding and calls upon all of a teacher's resources and professionalism.

To create the conditions that will foster excellent, progressive teachers does not need to be expensive, require years of training or the overhauling of curricula. What teachers need in order to teach well in a progressive system and to be fully engaged in it is relatively simple: autonomy in curriculum, assessment and decisions affecting them; to feel valued by society (respect and trust); and a culture of collaboration with enough time for planning. Teachers who work under these conditions will generally feel and exhibit a high degree of professionalism.[105]

These three conditions have been identified by the PISA studies, among others, as the conditions that lead to the highest teacher job satisfaction and the greatest educational outcomes.[106] They are certainly vitally important for progressive teaching to occur. This chapter will look at these and other conditions that allow teachers to give their best to their students, the factors that currently work against these conditions, and what the education system can do to overcome them.

AUTONOMY IN DECISION MAKING, CURRICULUM AND ASSESSMENT

Although I have taught in many schools, I spent most of my teaching career at Halifax Independent School, which started out its independent life as a cooperative. In its earliest years, all three or four teachers were on the board of directors, along with an equal number of parents plus one. This gave teachers a great deal of control over decisions on everything ranging from curriculum to finances. Policies were developed as needed, and were carefully crafted to reflect the unique needs of the school.

Salaries reflected what we could afford, which was often as low as 70 per cent of what teachers in the public system were getting. Some more business-minded observers questioned the wisdom of having teachers as part of the group that would decide on salaries and benefits, feeling that it created an inherent conflict of interest. What actually happened during these years of planning and building the new school was that the parent members of the board would consistently argue for higher salaries, while the teacher members, who perhaps appreciated more clearly the financial situation, would consistently advocate salary freezes. When the school finally got its new building and started to expand, attracting new teachers and keeping them became an issue, and salaries started to rise until they reached approximately 90 per cent of those in the public system. Teachers at Halifax Independent School had almost total autonomy over decisions that affected the school and their role within it, and it was an exciting place to teach.

When teachers have autonomy over what and how they teach, instead of being obliged to follow a set curriculum, it is amazing how creative and engaged they become. I have known teachers who would not have described themselves as innovative or creative when they started, but who after a few years at Halifax Independent School were developing highly original units of study. The example of others, the mentoring of more experienced teachers and the freedom to share ideas is motivating for teachers, as it is in other jobs.

Teachers at Halifax Independent are also responsible for creating and administering all student assessment, as we saw in Chapter 7. When an education system takes away the discretion of teachers over testing and curriculum, it is a way of "deskilling" them. Like most teachers, I was attracted to teaching partly by the opportunity to be creative in planning lessons and designing curriculum materials; teaching only ready-made content and lessons feels boring, frustrating and demeaning for most teachers. Using the authentic assessment measures we had developed as a group gave us confidence in our judgment, provided opportunities for real connection with our students and made us feel autonomous.

Pasi Sahlberg talks about the autonomy given to Finnish teachers:

> *They control curriculum, student assessment, school improvement and community involvement. Much as teachers around the world enter the profession with a mission to build community and transmit culture . . . Finnish teachers, in contrast to their peers in so many countries, have the latitude to follow through.*[107]

One of the key characteristics of the Finnish system, which Sahlberg points out, is the idea of the teacher as researcher. All teachers have a master's degree in education, which implies a familiarity with educational research and experience in conducting original research of their own. This allows them to benefit from new research-based ideas and methodologies, which they are then encouraged to try out.

On the other hand, in Britain, the highly centralized and standardized curriculum and testing leaves little room for teachers' creativity or initiative, and this, along with experiencing the deafness of the administration to their concerns, means that most teachers have little autonomy. The UK now has one of the worst records in the developed world for teacher recruitment and retention. Almost 50 per cent of teachers leave the profession after five years, despite having relatively good salaries and benefits.

The assessment of teachers is another area in which teachers themselves can play a role, both in developing the assessment system, as they do at Halifax Independent, and in carrying it out. The further away the assessor is in status to the one being assessed, the less autonomy the teacher feels. Thus, when teachers are assessed primarily by their peers, the feedback is more likely to contribute to their confidence as teachers instead of undermining it, as when they are assessed by "superiors." When teachers are evaluated by a principal or head teacher, who is considered part of a team of teachers instead of management, again, the feedback is more likely to be well received. On top of the stressful assessment that children in Britain go through (which also affects teachers), teachers there have to put up with assessments of their schools every four years or so, in which outside inspectors are free to barge into classrooms at any time. It is no wonder the job satisfaction rate among British teachers is so low!

The more autonomy we can give teachers over decision making, curriculum and assessment, the more we are likely to encourage true excellence in teaching. The contradiction in GERM countries is that by undermining teacher autonomy and trust, they actually limit themselves to a very narrow definition of teacher excellence that doesn't improve the student outcomes they are so concerned about.

RESPECT AND TRUST

> *"If you can hire people whose passion intersects with the job, they won't require any supervision at all. They will manage themselves better than anyone could ever manage them. Their fire comes from within, not from without. Their motivation is internal, not external."*
>
> — *Steven Covey*[108]

My experience has taught me that nearly all people who are treated with respect and are expected to be professional respond to those expectations to the best of their abilities. Teaching, as a career, tends to attract people who want to make a difference in the world, who have a strong commitment to children and their learning and who are invested in improving their own teaching practice. Of course, being a good teacher requires more than just having good intentions, but even if there were problems in the classroom, at Halifax Independent School everyone would work hard to overcome them. Some teachers needed support; when it was given in a respectful manner, those teachers grew and many became excellent teachers. I firmly believe that good teachers are not born, they are made — in large part by mentorship from more experienced teachers who have retained their enthusiasm for teaching.

In general, Canadian teachers enjoy respect and relatively good working conditions compared with many countries in the world. Canada ranks sixth out of the developed countries in terms of starting salaries for teachers[109] and most teachers have enjoyed the good benefits and working conditions that come along with the strong teacher associations to which they belong. Since 1920, the Canadian Teachers Federation has been an umbrella organization and powerful voice for the various provincial and territorial associations and unions that represent teachers. Canadian teachers also generally benefit from good training (for many provinces a teacher's degree requires two years of post-graduate study and practice teaching) and have many opportunities for professional development.

But these conditions are just a starting point. As I saw at Halifax Independent School, salaries, after a certain level has been reached, are not the most important factor — respect and trust are.

In Finland, "Teachers are autonomous in their work, as the system is based on trust rather than control."[110] The lack of standardized tests until the end of high school means that parents trust teachers' assessments, and trust them to do their jobs. Sahlberg describes the "shared responsibility" that happens when teachers work closely together for the school improvement that is a constant refrain. "Teachers have accepted curriculum development, experimentation with teaching methods, responsibility to engage in student welfare support, and collaboration with parents as important aspects of their work outside of classrooms."[111]

Canadian teachers also need to feel valued and trusted. However, the influences from GERM have begun to creep up on them and this has had an effect on the public's perception. Sometimes in the Canadian media, teachers have been portrayed as spoiled (long holidays, pension plans), as lazy and needing threats to make them work or as chronic complainers (too many special needs kids, too big classes, not enough resources).

GERM started with the perception that Western education systems were lagging behind the more rigorous Asian ones, and that our economies would soon follow suit if nothing was done. They blamed teachers, with their supposedly wishy-washy ideas about "child-centred" education. Part of the solution was to find ways to make teachers more "accountable" for their students' results, but this meant removing curriculum development and then the assessment of it from the teachers, and evaluating them more stringently. This sent the message that teachers were not to be trusted to do any of these things.

This lack of trust in teachers' judgment and expertise has now percolated right through the system. I remember one anxious parent who was worried about her eight-year-old's spelling, and who, in spite of reassurances on the part of several teachers that the child was a good, average speller for her age, insisted on taking her to a private tutoring agency for "testing." When the results came back that she was "above grade level," the parent was satisfied, but I thought that the whole episode was harmful to everyone — to the parent who needlessly spent extra money, to the teacher who felt demoralized and to the child who bore the brunt of the parent's anxiety.

At Halifax Independent School, parents put a great deal of trust in the teachers. Even though the governing board has more parents than teachers, teachers are generally deferred to on matters concerning curriculum and children's development. Parents see their role on the board as advisors or helpers; the teachers strive to be worthy of the trust that is put in them. Thus an atmosphere of "shared responsibility" is created, where the teachers help and monitor each other and the parents contribute where they have expertise.

When teachers are respected and teaching as a profession is highly valued, it becomes high status and more people want to get into it. Teaching in Finland is a highly sought-after profession, on the order of medicine, law or engineering. There are more than ten applicants for every opening in teacher education programs, and standards for admission are high. When teachers graduate with a master's degree and enter the profession, the high status keeps them in the field; 90 percent of Finnish teachers remain in education for the whole of their career. At Halifax Independent School, where teachers are respected and trusted, they tend to stay for a long time — many for more than twenty years.

A CULTURE OF COLLABORATION

Creating a culture of collaboration between teachers, administrators and parents is another key contributor to successful education. At Halifax Independent School, during its years as a cooperative, collaboration among teachers and parents was constant and expected. From regular meetings where teachers shared curriculum ideas, to committees of parents and teachers formed to develop policies, few decisions were made that were not collaborative. Learning activities such as Mini-Society would not have been possible without such collaboration, as well as the planning time needed.

As the children were coming in from the playground after recess, Heather, one of the Olds teachers, noticed some of the girls were teary eyed; a couple of others had grim, defiant expressions on their faces. While the rest of the class was gathering in the circle area, she pulled Lindsey and Jan aside and asked if everything was all right. Jan burst into tears, and Lindsey explained that Lily was being mean to them on the playground, and that it had been going on for a long time. Since Lily was in another class, and Jan and Lindsey didn't seem willing to talk about it further, Heather realized that she wouldn't be able to deal with it right away. She comforted the two girls and told them she would look into it.

The upper elementary teachers were having a lunch meeting that day, so Heather asked the other teachers if they had noticed anything going on with Lily. It turned out that several children in other classes had mentioned that Lily and her two best friends were "being mean," but no one would be more specific. One teacher said she had overheard something being whispered about a "club," and wondered if that might have something to do with it. After comparing notes a little further, Heather was delegated to meet with Jan, Lindsey, Lily and her two best friends to get to the root of the problem, which she did before the end of lunchtime. It turned out that Lily had organized a secret club to which you could only belong if you played a trick on someone else. Some of the tricks were quite mean. Lindsey described how she had been asked to hide Jan's lunchbox, but didn't want to since she was her friend. Both girls had a chance to tell Lily how they felt about the situation, and after a lot of discussion, Heather felt that Lily understood the impact her exclusive, secret "club" was having on everyone else. She shared her results with the other teachers, who would all keep an eye on the girls to make sure there were no repeat occurrences, and who would all talk to their classes in general about playing tricks and excluding children.

> The collaboration between these teachers, who worked closely together on many issues and shared a common commitment to children's emotional health, was vital to nip this problem in the bud. Because it involved several classes and was "secret," the situation could very easily have gone unnoticed by the teachers and have escalated into a bullying situation. This is the kind of situation that arises often with children, and for which collaboration is essential. When there is no culture of collaboration, it will often be overlooked.

Teachers in Finland have a great deal of autonomy over curriculum, the life of the school and community involvement, and to exercise this, they collaborate together a great deal. But collaboration between teachers and with parents requires time, which needs to be built into the school day. Finnish primary children have only 650 hours per year of instructional time (590 in middle school) compared with 900 for Canadian children and 1080 hours for Americans. This allows ample time for collaboration and for the preparation that is necessary for schools where there is no set curriculum.

Teachers in Canada are already spending about as much time working and preparing outside the classroom as in it (an average work week of forty-nine hours means about twenty-five hours "instructional time" and twenty-four hours preparation).[112] "Teacher burn out" is often a big topic at teacher and principal professional development sessions. Teacher collaboration time needs to be built into the school week — time for peer assessments, curriculum planning, mentorship and professional development.

More hours of instructional time does not necessarily lead to better outcomes on tests or any other measures of education. I cringe when I hear a news story about schools in the US cancelling recess or otherwise lengthening the school day or year to increase teaching time, on the theory that this will boost student achievement. This flies in the face of all the research on the subject. Students need breaks; in Finland, they get breaks every forty-five minutes. Teachers also perform better when they have ample time for collaboration and preparation, and when they are not working late into the night and on weekends. Many countries give children an afternoon off per week to provide time for teacher collaboration; others have a shorter school day so that after-school meetings and preparation do not keep teachers at school into the evenings. This would be worthwhile for Canadian schools to consider.

Creating a culture of collaboration requires trust, respect and teacher autonomy as well as dedicated time in the week. However, there are some structural factors that actively work against collaboration. When the system encourages teachers to compete against each other, which is what happens when external rewards are used to incentivize individuals, it is not surprising that collaboration will suffer. In both the US and Britain, some administrators have claimed that the best way to encourage excellence in teachers is to reward it with "merit pay." In many schools in the US, the Value Added Model is used to measure a class's "growth" in scores over the school year and as a way to sort out what gains or losses are caused by the teacher, as opposed to other factors such as absenteeism or socio-economic status. This model has many problems and, the author of one study concluded: "If anything, teacher incentives may decrease student achievement, especially in larger schools."[113]

Even if one could measure teacher effectiveness fairly and objectively, the singling out of "good" teachers for rewards leads to dysfunctional competition among teachers, exactly the opposite of the PISA findings on collaboration among teachers. Teachers will often choose to plan alone, so that they will get all the credit for successful activities.

Assessment of teachers should not be used to reward the good and punish the bad, but to provide support and encouragement for all teachers to help them improve their practice. At Halifax Independent, where sharing is encouraged, teachers feel rewarded when others want to emulate something they have tried.

Teacher autonomy, respect and collaboration are three basic conditions that have been shown to actually improve student learning, and they are absolutely essential for any kind of progressive teaching. But there are other conditions that are also important for progressive teaching and for which many teachers have been advocating for years. One of these is keeping class size and composition to levels at which teachers feel they can teach the way they know is best for children.

CLASS SIZE AND COMPOSITION

More students in a class means more administrative work for teachers: more report cards, more marking, more parent contact and therefore less time for planning and one-on-one attention. One of the most contentious and, for parents, confusing issues is that of class size and the numbers of special needs children in those classes (the polite term for which is "class composition"). Much has been written about it, and recently it has been one of the main issues in negotiations between teachers and governments.

Teachers care about student learning, and about the wellbeing of their students. They know that with large classes they can't give children the individual attention they need, both for their emotional wellbeing and for their academic progress.

If you have read this far in this book, you will have an appreciation for the amount of individual attention that is required for progressive teaching to work, and why Halifax Independent School caps its elementary classes at eighteen (and middle school at twenty-two). But if you take a look at the extensive literature on the subject, you will see that there is a huge and confusing variety of studies on the subject of class size, with very contradictory results. In Canada, a paper issued by the CD Howe Institute in 2005, "School Class Size: Smaller isn't Better,"[114] received a great deal of media coverage and has influenced governments, even though many of its conclusions were questioned. It bases its findings upon studies by economists, such as Hanushek,[115] who are concerned about costs arising from lowering class size, and who use students' results on standardized tests as their only measure of achievement.

So what is going on here? Who can we believe? If raising test scores were the only goal of education, then it probably doesn't matter how many children are taught by one teacher — I can prepare thirty-five children just as well as twenty children if all I am doing is vertical, whole-class teaching aimed at drilling the answers to standardized test questions.

However, recent research and many older, well-established studies look at variables other than test scores to measure outcomes, such as number of interactions between teachers and students, attitudes toward learning, long-term educational attainment and teacher satisfaction. What is not in question is that research has shown that smaller classes (especially under twenty students) are very beneficial for students in the early years. Even the CD Howe report acknowledges this effect for Kindergarten and Grade 1, and attributes it to the fact that these years are largely about "socialization." I guess the underlying assumption here is that social learning stops at the age of six and that the rest of schooling is only about passing tests.

These studies point out that with smaller classes, "there was more individual attention, a more active role for the pupils, and beneficial effects on the quality of teaching."[116] These positive effects are even stronger for children who have been "educationally disadvantaged,"[117] and for classes where "innovative" teaching styles such as self-reporting grades, formative evaluation and "micro-teaching" are used.[118]

HOW CAN WE KEEP TEACHERS ENGAGED?

> *"I love my job! You learn something new everyday. Today's lesson: my car can fit five Christmas trees. Who knew?!?"*
> — *Liam Knox, Middles Teacher (Facebook)*

Parents want their children to spend their days with teachers who know their children and are excited about learning — in other words, are engaged. Teachers want to be engaged and want the best for the children they teach. Therefore it seems logical that one of the essential cornerstones of a healthy, progressive education system is to make sure teachers get what they need to do their jobs.

Yet in many places we still have unhappy teachers and parents. We have looked at the effects of GERM on teachers, and seen how it undermines the three major characteristics of a healthy teaching force (feeling valued, having autonomy

Shop stewards at a union meeting.

and having time for collaboration), and it is foolish to think that Canadian education is immune from these influences.

When Halifax Independent was starting to grow and we were building the new school, there were times when the stress level among teachers was quite high. We were constantly having evening meetings to make decisions about the direction of the school, meeting with builders and architects, fundraising, developing new policies and recruiting new students — and this when all of us had full teaching schedules! The staff had recently doubled in size, and some of us noticed that not everyone felt as free to express concerns as others did. When things settled down after we moved in to the new building, we decided do an anonymous staff survey, as well as a parent one. Both were very revealing, but what really stood out was the number of hours the teachers worked each week (it ranged from forty-eight to sixty), and the worry they felt over how this was affecting their families.

Recognizing that this state of affairs was not sustainable, the staff and some parents sat down to figure out what to do about it. We came up with a much more realistic division of labour, streamlining the number of teacher meetings, and mandating only one teacher on each parent committee instead of several. As a staff, we also became more conscious of the need for work/life balance and reminded each other of it from time to time. These surveys were repeated every two years, and always gave us something new to work on — a good example of how shared responsibility can contribute to a constantly improving, vital institution.

Halifax Independent continued to operate as a cooperative long after it gave up its official designation. This structure allowed us to keep a focus on everyone's needs, children, parents and teachers, but acknowledged that teachers do matter a lot. In order to have truly excellent teachers, we made sure that they felt listened to, respected and had lots of time to work together.

OUT OF AUTONOMY COMES CREATIVITY

> *"It's a glimpse of the real world — you don't always get the stall you want on Market Day."*
> *— ten-year-old student about Mini-Society*

Think back to the most memorable "best school" experiences from your school days, moments where you felt you had surmounted a barrier or discovered something brand new, or perhaps just felt the warmth of being a part of a cohesive team. Chances are that those experiences were not during regular classes. It was likely memorable because it was not part of the daily school experience. The sad thing is that schools are not

Depositing money in the Middle School bank.

providing enough of these memorable experiences, and when they do, they are usually outside the classroom.

Holistic learning situations that involve many classes and take up large chunks of classroom time can be some of the deepest, most satisfying and memorable experiences of school. When teachers have the autonomy, encouraged by supportive parents, to plan these unique learning situations and have the opportunity and mandate to carry them out, they will rise to the challenge. When they have years to collaborate and fine-tune these opportunities, the results are worth sharing. Having a flexible, made-in-school curriculum greatly facilitates the sense of ownership that enriches both the teachers and the children.

One such extended, integrated whole-school activity developed at Halifax Independent School is Mini-Society. It, like the Plays described in Chapter 4, has solid pedagogical goals and allows children the chance to learn through doing something real. In fact, both activities are exactly the sort of "waste of time" activities that a school focused on maximizing standardized test scores would cut, but actually they teach valuable social and artistic skills, as well as literacy and numeracy.

> On a hot day in June, the whole student population is crammed into the lunchroom. Children are seated on the floor and crowded on the benches. Teachers are sprinkled throughout the throng, sometimes redirecting a child's attention to the front of the room, where several teachers are leading a discussion. The topic of discussion: workers' compensation and sick pay.
>
> Eleven-year-old Ellen describes what happened the day before, while she was making a snack during Mini-Society, "I went to sit down at the table to peel apples. Somebody bumped into the table and it collapsed on my leg. A sharp part cut my knee. It was bleeding a lot, and I had to go see Valerie. I missed the rest of the session getting cleaned up. They thought I might need stitches, but I didn't."
>
> The teacher asks, "It must have hurt. But why are you bringing it up here?"
>
> "Because, I didn't get paid for the time I missed. And it's not fair!"
>
> "What do people think about this?" asks the teacher.
>
> "On Monday I missed school because I was sick, and I didn't get paid either!" adds eight-year-old Nick indignantly.
>
> "Why should we pay people who don't work?" wonders another teacher. "If we start doing that, we will lose a lot of money."
>
> "My mum says that in the real world, people get paid when they are sick or hurt," Ellen says. "We should get sick pay!"
>
> A chorus of "it's not fair!" and "if workers aren't treated well, they can refuse to work" ensues. After a few minutes, it is agreed that the students need a union meeting to decide on a course of action. The five union leaders (aged eight to eleven) come to the front of the

> room, and take over the meeting, while the teachers step outside. When the teachers return to the room, they listen to some demands from the "union reps," and after a little more discussion, they agree to institute half pay for children who are sick or hurt, retroactively. The children file out, faces pink from heat and excitement, eagerly discussing their union victory. A strike has been averted!

What is happening here? Are children being paid to go to school? Since when have they been unionized? The answer to all the above is that this is the week when the whole school is literally turned into a "mini society," with everyone participating in a huge week-long simulation game. Mini-Society turns teachers into bosses and children into workers, allowing them all to explore the World of Work in a hands-on way. During the first four days of the week, the children are workers, producing goods to be sold and getting paid a wage (in a made-up currency) to do it. Daily meetings allow children to explore a range of workplace issues such as equity, benefits, savings, workers' rights and currency issues. Mini-Society culminates in a Market Day on Friday morning, when the school is transformed into a marketplace with stalls selling various handmade items, food concessions, games, spas, buskers, paid advertising and mobile vendors. At the end of the week, the children reflect on what they have earned and learned, taking home their goods, leftover "money" and ideas for next year's Mini-Society.

Did we learn about unions in social studies at school? If I did, I have long forgotten it, along with a lot about imports and exports to various countries. That's because most of what I learned in social studies was from a textbook. These young denizens of Mini-Society are actually experiencing firsthand some of the reasons unions were formed in the first place. The feelings and insights they experience from the discussions will live with them for a long time.

How does Mini-Society work?

The week before Mini-Society starts, the all-important detail of the name of the currency for this year is discussed and voted on by all the students in the school. It always amazes me that names such as "googoogagas," "dylonges" or "oodles" roll off the tongue so easily after a few days of use. Once the currency name has been decided, the older students create designs for the different denominations and stacks of coloured, photocopied bills are produced, ready to be handed over to the Mini-Society "bank," run by middle school students. On Monday morning, the day starts with a whole-school meeting, where the elementary children are divided into five multi-class producer groups and reminded of some of the basic elements of Mini-Society. They are told that they will be paid twelve oodles (or whatever) for their work from 9:00 to 10:30 each day (and one afternoon). The five workplaces are Snack, Newspaper, two Craft areas and Gardening. On Friday they will have a chance to buy some of the crafts from a "warehouse" at wholesale prices and resell them during the marketplace, as well as items that they have made at home. They are told that after work time is over (at snack time), they will be able to deposit their money in the Mini-Society bank, thus gaining interest over the week of 10 per cent per day. Then they are reminded to be sure to save out some oodles to buy the snack (produced by the Snack group) and the newspaper.

Then off the various groups go to their workplaces, where they work with one or two teachers to make their product. Just before 10:30, the bosses pay the salaries to the workers;

sometimes, to the shock of a few children, pay is docked for individuals not working hard enough or bonuses are given for work beyond the call of duty. Next, the children line up to deposit their earnings in the bank (the five branches are conveniently located outside each classroom workplace and staffed by middle school students). Outside the lunchroom, vendors are hawking their version of the daily newspaper, hot off the presses, so that children have something to read as they munch on the daily snack, purchased from a stall within the lunchroom. Then, all the children run outside to be children again, ready to start all over the next morning in a different activity. Over the four mornings and one afternoon, all children experience each workplace and get paid for five "days" of work.

After playtime each day, a whole-school Meeting reinforces some of the details of how Mini-Society works, as well as deals with issues that arise during the sessions. The younger children are often confused about what happens on Market Day and don't understand why it's a good idea to trust their hard-earned cash to the banks. Stories of lost or stolen money, as well as the advantages of earning interest are shared, but it always surprises me that some children refuse to patronize the banks and prefer their pockets instead. Issues of fairness or equity are raised: one year a student pointed out that another group was dismissed fifteen minutes early, but still got paid as much as the others. Another year teachers forgot what the rate of pay the previous year was, and salaries were set at a lower rate: a union was formed to agitate for higher pay. The system of handing out bonuses is often considered to be arbitrary by the children, and lots of discussion ensues about how to make it fairer. Since fairness is important to children, these discussions happen every year and are remembered from one year to the next.

What is actually produced during these work sessions? In the Snack group, the children make healthy but fun snacks designed to appeal to their peers, and then sell them for two oodles at snack time. A small group produces a roving commercial that visits all the other workplaces, singing a jingle or acting out a skit — for example, chanting "Chocolate covered pretzels, curly and delicious!"

In the Newspaper group, children brainstorm and are assigned various topics on which to report, and then are dispatched with clipboards to conduct interviews, polls and observations of what is happening in Mini-Society that day. They are given a strict deadline in which to return so that they can edit and finish their good copy in time. Comics, games and puzzles are drawn and a name is chosen for each paper. By Wednesday or Thursday, ads are solicited (at a price) to promote some of the businesses that will be appearing at the Marketplace on Friday. It can get very hectic toward 10:30, when the competing pressures of uncooperative photocopiers, unmet deadlines, a public clamouring for their daily read and employees needing to be paid can result in some palpitations on the part of the editors. But it is all worth it for the sight of a room full of children absorbed in reading their papers while munching on the snack of the day.

A variety of items are produced in the two Craft groups each day. Most often the craft is something that can be made by children of all ages and is appealing for children and adults alike. Friendship bracelets, hand-made diaries, mandalas, bubbleprint cards, origami animals, games, toys and painted rocks are just a few of the items that have been produced. Sometimes a Craft group produces something that has a real and practical use for the school. When the school was hosting a fundraising run, the children became button producers, and designed and made buttons to give out as participation medals. When the native garden needed a fence built to protect it from soccer balls (and players), a Craft session became a Fence Factory, where each child painted a fence picket. These were later assembled and installed into a colourful, funky picket fence that the children enjoy every day on the playground. But the main purpose of the Craft sessions is to produce items that can then be bought and sold on Market Day.

The Gardening group performs a real service. The children help with planting and weeding in the vegetable or native garden, as well as pruning and labelling various crops. On rainy days, they create garden crafts to be sold on Market Day — painted plant pots, child-designed packets of seeds, bottle birdfeeders or concrete paving stones to name a few.

Friday morning, or Market Day, is easily the most exciting, eagerly anticipated day of the school year. Some children plan what they are going to do months in advance. A few days before, all the children have had an opportunity to buy a license for the particular business they and their friends are going to have. Food licenses are very popular, so there is a lottery to decide who gets them. Mobile vending licenses (the right to use the trolley carts from the kitchen) are also popular, and as there are only two of them, a lottery is often needed there too. Gaming licenses are issued, as well as busking licenses and licenses for retail outlets.

Market Day starts as the children withdraw all their money from the bank and then are called down in groups, according to a lottery system, to buy goods from the craft

WHAT TEACHERS NEED: AUTONOMY, TRUST AND A CULTURE OF COLLABORATION 239

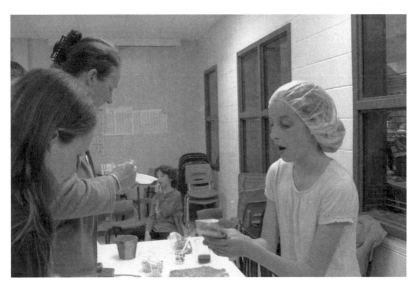

Selling treats at the Mini-Society market.

"warehouse." Items are grouped in batches of two or three, with a price designed to reflect the amount of work put into them — some items are made by one child alone in a session, while others are the work of several children together. This is the time where many children need an explanation why they can't just buy the one item that they made themselves, and some need to be encouraged to "spend money to make money." Younger ones often need some counselling on what sort of markup on the items they buy will allow them to make money, but not price themselves out of the market. If sales in the warehouse are not brisk enough, the teachers will reduce the wholesale price in order to stimulate the economy, and get the goods to market.

While all this is going on, the other children are setting up their shops in classrooms around the school, displaying licenses and making price tags. The lunchroom is set aside as a Food Market, and all vendors are anxiously awaiting the warehouse to close so that they can set up. As soon as it is closed, the blenders come out and the trays of cupcakes and cookies are attractively displayed. At 9:30, the Market is declared open for business, and the school starts to buzz.

> **Market Day**
>
> As five-year-olds, Jennie, Marcy and Celine travel around the school with Celine's mother, Adrienne, they come across a girl lying on the floor with her legs wrapped around her neck, and a hat out for donations. The girls watch in fascination for a few minutes as the busker unwinds herself, and then performs a perfect cartwheel down the hall. Adrienne points out the hat, and asks if anyone would like to give her some money. Jennie and Marcy each place an oodle in the hat, but Celine clings to her mother's hand and refuses. They hear the blare of music coming from a classroom at the top of the stairs, and, following the scent of nail polish, they enter the "spa" room. A reclining chair is inhabited by a relaxed teacher who is getting a "deluxe head massage." Jars of colourful nail polish deck every available surface, and all eight of the operators are busy painting garish and varied nails on young customers, over half of whom are boys. The girls get their nails done, seated in small chairs around a white school table, and are pleased by the effect of their ten shiny fingernails, each painted a different colour. They pay their two oodles, and Celine is delighted that when she hands over a five oodle note, she gets three notes back in return.
>
> Travelling down the hall, they encounter a violin player busking, but don't stop there. Adrienne shepherds the group through classroom after classroom, visiting each shop in turn. The girls are anxious to spend the rest of their thirty oodles. They stop and make guesses on the number of gummy worms in a jar, and experiment with some paper airplanes made by Olaf. The chime of the intercom blings, and a loud voice declares, "Come outside the back door to the middle school gagaball game! Only four oodles a turn!"

> The girls stop and take a few turns trying to toss a ring over the noses of Harry Potter figures painted on a board, and then watch some card tricks performed by a magician in a top hat (Adrienne is not sure if the girls appreciate fully the magic in their card suddenly appearing on the top of the pile). They walk past a stall selling origami Star Wars characters and another with pictures from a popular video game, but spend most of their time looking at all the goods on offer at several "craft" shops. Friendship bracelets, necklaces made from beads and washers and painted flower pots are all fingered and compared. One stall has a lovely felted bird that was one of only about ten made in a craft group, and Adrienne thinks that Celine might like to buy it. With prompting, Celine asks the eight-year-old vendor its cost, and is told, "forty-five oodles."
>
> Her mother gasps, "Wow, that is expensive!" The vendor shrugs, "I don't really want to sell it — I'm keeping it to give to my mother."
>
> They move on. Adrienne helps each girl decide what to buy, and soon they have spent almost all their oodles, saving only a few for a visit to the food market. After buying cupcakes with gummy worms crawling on top, Adrienne and the girls head back to their classroom. They flop on the carpet with their purchases, showing them to the other children. Soon, the announcement comes that Market Day is over. The class gathers up their purchases, tidies up their shops and heads off to snack. Some have leftover oodles, which they stuff into pockets, one proudly proclaiming, "I have twenty oodles left over. I'm going to take them home to play store with my brother."

Meeting: A time to debrief

The big Meeting, after Market Day is over and the children have had a chance to blow off steam outside for a while, is always a lively affair, and often takes up the rest of the morning. Issues about what happened are brought up and discussed, grievances are heard, questions are answered and suggestions are made about things that could be done differently next year. One Meeting, Marianne put up her hand, upset that when she bought six tickets in a raffle and her name was picked, she was disqualified because the seven-year-old seller said, "It's not fair that her name was in there six times and everyone else only had one." After some discussion, in which other children weighed in, explaining the inherent unfairness from Marianne's perspective (that she had paid for six tickets, and therefore deserved to have them all considered), the problem was turned over to a teacher, who settled it privately with the two children.

"Why is Market Day so short? I didn't have time to do any shopping, I was so busy selling!" was the next comment. Many children echoed this, and some of the teachers agreed that it did seem rather short this year (one hour). Other children suggested strategies for dealing with this perennial problem: having a business partner, and then taking turns minding the shop; or if you are by yourself, just putting a "Closed" sign up when you want to go shopping.

"What happens to our leftover oodles?" Because the children badly want there to be a purpose for earning lots of oodles, the teachers will often allow their classes to pool their leftover oodles, and buy them back in exchange for "free time" during class time. This year one child suggested that they be allowed to save their oodles until next year's Mini-Society, and then exchange them for the new currency (at a sharply reduced rate). A lively discussion ensued about what this would mean for Mini-Society, and many agreed that it could change it profoundly. The teachers said that they would think about it for next year, but that if there was such a change it should happen then. In the meantime, oodles had no monetary value.

The big Meeting with all the children can only deal with a small number of issues before restlessness, heat or lunchtime puts an end to it. But the experience has provided fodder for discussion at the class level, and many of the most interesting discussions happen there. When the older children meet in their class group, more complex issues are explored, such as taxing workers to pay for social services like sick pay, the concept of contributing to the public good (working in the school gardens) and the possibility of being paid a fraction of their worth for leftover oodles the following year. In the younger classes, time is often spent explaining some of the decisions made in the big meeting. For instance, many of the young children could not understand why Marianne felt hard done by when she was told she couldn't win the lottery; in their minds it didn't seem fair that she had six chances while others only had one.

Mini-Society changes over time and requires much planning and collaboration on the part of teachers

Mini-Society is not a static event. It has been going for over twenty-five years at Halifax Independent School, but each year there is a different theme, sometimes initiated by teachers, and at other times driven by the children themselves. One year, Donny insisted that Mini-Society needed a police force (someone had lost some oodles and was sure they had been stolen). Teachers resisted this idea, saying that Mini-Society was founded on principles of trust and honesty — that it did not fully reflect the real world in every respect. The next year, Donny led a group of children in a daring bank heist in which they "kidnapped" the money supply from the head teacher's office — it was some time and a special meeting before the perpetrators were identified, and their demands made known. They wanted to show that a police force really was needed!

Another year, a group of children decided that they weren't being paid enough, and paraded around with signs demanding more money. Teachers conferred, told the children that they couldn't deal with rabble like that, and suggested that they form a union and send some representatives to present their demands to the "bosses." Thus was the first union born, and for several years thereafter, time was given in the day for union organization. Representatives were chosen from each group, and meetings were held in the various "locals," as well as between shop stewards and the bosses.

One spring, after unions had been established in Mini-Society for a year or two, there was a particularly protracted and bitter strike in Halifax at the phone company, in which picket lines were visible all over the city. When Mini-Society started a few days later, a group of older students, who had talked to some of the striking workers while on a walk, tried to whip up the rest of the children into taking strike action over a somewhat trumped-up issue. The union put it to a vote, and the strike was voted down, whereupon this group decided to hold their own strike anyway. They made signs, and marched around in front of the school, much to the bemusement of the other children. Teachers refused their requests and encouraged the union to levy fines on them — much discussion ensued about wildcat strikes and the importance of honouring the democratic process. Emotions ran very high, and it took several days for the main actors, with teacher help, to resolve the issues. It was remarkably similar to what can happen in a real strike!

At the same time, teachers felt that after doing Mini-Society for six or seven years, many middle schoolers were ready for a change, so they were taken out of the regular rotation and now take part in various simulation games or projects designed to further their financial literacy. They still run the bank, design the currency and are full and enthusiastic participants in Market Day, though.

> **Pickle Juice**
>
> Every year, there are a few businesses that garner extra attention, either because they are so popular and make a lot of oodles, or because they show such ingenuity that they often fundamentally change the way Mini-Society works.
>
> One year, a group of five upper elementary boys formed a consortium, called themselves the "Pickles," and applied for a food license. Their plan, it seemed, was to bring food and drink items from home, sell them and make a fortune. What was different with this group was that they had a novel approach to selling: instead of making price tags for the various items, they asked of each potential customer, "What do you want to pay?"
>
> As Nico put it, "If we put down the prices on papers, then they would only pay that price."
>
> It turned out, especially as the morning went on, that some children wanted to pay a lot. Younger children especially would often offer ten or fifteen oodles, instead of the two or three that was the usual rate. Toward the end of the morning, as children were realizing that they had money that had to be spent, and that some popular items were getting scarce, the Pickles started the practice of auctioning items off. One jollypop (a homemade sucker) sold for one hundred oodles. Nico bought three cupcakes from his little sister because they weren't selling, ate one and then sold the other two for eighty oodles each.
>
> Colin said, "If people are willing to pay more, why should we object? The best customers were the Middles, because they were

a little careless with money. But they were overjoyed when they went away!"

The other innovative thing about the Pickles group is that they sold shots of pickle juice (again, pay what you want) to be drunk to the cheers of the bystanders. Colin explained it this way, "I got my brother in Olds to say he would do it (he actually likes pickle juice), and he told all his friends ahead of time. We created a certain amount of hype, so we had a guaranteed customer base when we started." They did a roaring trade in shots of pickle juice, until a teacher came along and suggested that if a younger child were to drink it and vomit, it would be the Pickles' responsibility to clean it up. After weighing the risks, the group decided to shut down this part of the operation.

When it was all over, the group split their takings of 1360 oodles five ways, and were convinced that theirs was the most successful business. In the later discussion, Sebastian, the youngest member of the group, expressed some doubts about some of their business practices: "It was fun, but I didn't feel good about ripping off the Middles. We were taking too much money. I was afraid that if our prices were too high, the teachers would find out. And we lost the middle schoolers because our prices were too high."

Although not everyone agreed with him, they all acknowledged that at the end of the day the amount of money they made was not important — everyone had fun, and that was what counted.

What is being learned?

At its most basic level, and probably one of the reasons it was initially conceived, Mini-Society is a brilliant reinforcement of and opportunity to apply math skills learned throughout the year. The youngest children learn about counting money, about adding and subtracting when making change and about multiplication and division when making "fair shares."

WHAT TEACHERS NEED: AUTONOMY, TRUST AND A CULTURE OF COLLABORATION

Buying and selling.

As they get older, the mathematical operations get more complex as children enter into businesses with friends, and need to share expenses and profits, figure out a reasonable markup (if I buy three flower pots at the warehouse for fifteen oodles, what should I charge to sell them?) and work out how much interest, at 10 per cent, they will receive on their savings. Middle school students who run the bank are in charge of adding up all the children's deposits, figuring out the amount of interest owed and paying out the bank savings to all the children on Market Day.

The producer groups in which children participate each morning have solid pedagogical goals. The Craft groups promote artistic and fine motor skills, the Snack group learns about food safety and nutrition in addition to basic food preparation, the Newspaper reinforces literacy and working to deadlines and the Gardening group, in addition to practising some basic gardening skills, learns about the importance of contributing a service to the community.

Financial literacy is another skill fostered by Mini-Society. The idea of saving and gaining interest on the savings is the most elementary, but many higher order skills are also learned, like budgeting (don't forget to save out three oodles to buy snack and the newspaper!) and business planning (how much do we need for our licenses? Who will pay for advertising? Who will supply what? How much will we charge? How do we share our profits?). One seven-year-old boy, Josh, was slightly disgruntled that his partners only gave him ten oodles as his share of the profits from selling the plasticine figures that he had made at home. Upon further discussion, it emerged that he had spent most of Market Day playing gagaball, and hadn't actually sold any himself. Chatting with the boys involved elicited the suggestion that perhaps it would have been fairer if Josh had just sold the plasticine figures to his friends outright, who could then resell them, keeping the profits to themselves. Most children are very interested in fairness, and it seems that most of the business groups are cooperatively run, although the exceptions provide a great deal of meat for discussion.

The children learn and absorb consumer awareness through watching others and experiencing shopping transactions. A child who buys a bracelet from one stall, and then immediately spots the same item at another for half the price learns about comparative shopping. Items that are scarce force children to ask themselves, "How much am I willing to pay for this?" When Lalia bought a clay figurine that immediately disintegrated in her hand, she was encouraged to take it back and ask for a refund. Picture her dismay, when on returning, she found the stall closed up and the owner off spending his profits! Critical thinking happens when children see and hear advertising that is inaccurate or misleading (and it does happen, even though the assumption of honesty still applies).

Ethical issues are dealt with on a daily basis during Mini-Society, both in the big meetings and in discussions between children. Is it okay to overcharge (or rip off) younger children if they seem happy about it? Is it all right to display an object for sale, and then refuse to sell it to someone? What is a fair way to split profits or expenses when not everyone does an equal share of the work? Is it okay to sell something if you know it doesn't work? Through participating in this type of discussion, children develop the vocabulary and insight to analyze complex ethical and moral issues.

Philosophical questions come up frequently as children ask themselves, "What is the goal of Mini-Society (or life)?" What are they striving for? Is it only to get the most oodles or is there something more important to them? At the end of the week, some children experience a feeling of let-down; perhaps it is not a bad thing that they experience the fleetingness of material wealth when Market Day is all over, and their oodles are worthless.

One of the strengths of Mini-Society is that it happens every year, so that the children carry their insights from one year to the next, deepening and broadening their understanding. The children get a chance to fix and improve on things that didn't work, to try different business ideas and to view what happens through different lenses as they mature. It is fascinating to observe that the sophistication of both the discussions and the businesses increase as children get older, and to see the enthusiasm with which the children plan Mini-Society, sometimes months in advance.

Many parents try to instill financial responsibility in their children through giving them allowances, opening

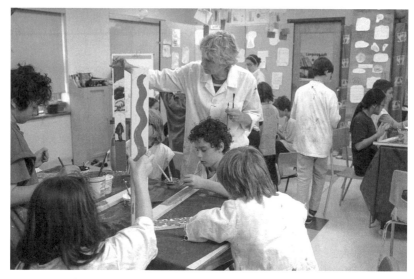

Making a fence for the native garden in Mini-Society.

bank accounts or assigning chores. The range of skills the children are learning in Mini-Society goes far beyond what parents can do on their own. Using the social group of the school allows for much more in-depth exploration of these issues, while at the same time the children are "meeting outcomes" in the math and literacy curricula.

But the bottom line is that Mini-Society is really just a more elaborate version of the lemonade stand. Most children are very happy to buy and sell, to have a product that others appreciate and to play at the adult world of money and marketing. If they have managed to buy something to take home with their own hard-earned money, and end up with a few oodles to play with, the week has been a success. Children learn through play and through imitation of the adult world, and this week is a celebration of that most precious part of childhood.

CONCLUSION

Is it possible that every child in Canada could say their school not only feels like the best school in the world, but that it actually is the best school for them? I think it is.

I believe that all parents want a school that brings out the best in their child, with teachers who appreciate their child in all their foibles, talents, charms and fragilities. I think that at the best school for each child, the fundamental relationship is between the "whole child" and their respected, trusted teacher. That relationship is deeply personal and when it is allowed to flourish, teachers can use their intelligence, training and experience to provide the opportunities that are uniquely suited for each child to learn in a way that keeps their love of learning intact, while they acquire the twenty-first-century skills they will need.

In this book, I have explored the many ways in which this relationship between children and teachers can flourish, as it does at Halifax Independent School. I have also discussed structural factors within education systems that conspire against it.

When teachers are bound by narrow, grade-specific curriculum outcomes, they constantly have to relegate what the children want to learn to second place. In that environment, teachers have to tell an excited child that their fascination with dinosaurs will have to wait until next year because dinosaurs are not on the Grade 1 curriculum. A narrow focus on delivering prescribed outcomes means that children are judged in terms of how they are meeting arbitrary deadlines at particular ages, and never seen as the "whole children" they are. Whole children — that is to say, real children — come with diverse learning styles, personalities, abilities and emotional needs, and they all develop at different rates.

At each stage of education, schools should be getting students ready for the next stage of the child's life. Children starting middle school need to be literate, eager to learn and have a broad base of skills — but does it matter if they learned to use a semi-colon properly in Grade 4 or Grade 6? In today's school system, many parents worry about their child "falling behind" when they are not meeting a specific outcome at a specific time. A child who has difficulty getting ideas down on paper in Grade 2 may not meet the Grade 2 outcome for writing. But I have seen children in that situation at Halifax Independent who, when they weren't made to feel they were somehow lacking, spontaneously started writing reams by the time they were in Grade 4.

With the smaller classes that are essential for hands-on learning, teachers can easily see when specific students need extra support. Resource teachers, if necessary, can then work as true assets in the classroom, and provide strategic help where and when it is needed.

In this book I have argued that it is dysfunctional to have centrally mandated curricula — unless the curricula are very general, and intended only as guidelines. A locally produced curriculum can be adjusted to be more authentic and responsive to children's interests and the real world they live in. Allowing some element of choice in what they learn ensures that children are motivated and engaged, and inspires the children to learn the skills they need to follow their interests. Why make a Grade 3 class wait until Grade

6 to learn about electricity, when they have just been studying simple machines and decide they want to electrify the machines they have built?

I am most familiar with the theme studies approach embraced by Halifax Independent School and have described its workings in some detail, but all progressive methodologies share the same commitment to hands-on learning. Hands-on learning, which research has shown is more effective for children's understanding and motivation, can be seen as an extension of the child's need for play. This does not disappear once a child starts school.

Hands-on learning is important for all areas of the curriculum, including mathematics. In schools like Halifax Independent, where hands-on math teaching emphasizes understanding and problem solving, students are interested and motivated, and they learn the basics without the boredom associated with pointless drills.

At Halifax Independent, with its locally focused curriculum, students learn the basic skills while at the same time learning content that is interesting to them. The first four Cs of the twenty-first-century skills, creativity, critical thinking, communication and collaboration, are integrated into every aspect of the curriculum. When authentic materials are used instead of standard textbooks and "units of study," there is the ongoing need to examine sources, so critical thinking becomes embedded. Media literacy has become an essential subset of critical thinking skills in this age of exploding social media, fake news and "post-truth" politics. Collaboration, communication and creativity are much more likely to happen organically when teachers are freed from the constraints of a prescriptive curriculum.

At Halifax Independent the arts are emphasized, both

in specialist classes and integrated into theme studies. All children deserve the chance to participate in arts and music activities, and for many children this is when they have those "best school" moments. Musical theatre, like the annual Plays at Halifax Independent, is an excellent way of giving children an integrated, truly immersive experience in the arts. Cutbacks in education budgets cannot be justified by calling arts education a "frill" — it is an essential component of the curriculum for whole children.

Using the theme or project-based approach to second language teaching, and integrating it with topics children are learning about in their regular classes capitalizes on the motivation of students at Halifax Independent. It also enriches their vocabulary, and expands on their knowledge. Unfortunately, many of the resources for language teaching in Canada are put into early French immersion programs, and these are not available to all who could benefit from them. Considering the multitude of advantages of knowing another language, as well as some of the problems associated with early immersion programs, I made the case for more intensive, hands-on, project-based French programs that start at a later age and are universal.

At Halifax Independent School, where teachers are not bound by centrally mandated curricula and the stresses of frequent standardized tests, they can daily integrate the development of curiosity, caring and discovering one's capabilities, the last three Cs of twenty-first-century skills. The hidden curriculum or climate of the school is such that children learn that their teacher genuinely cares about them and that everyone is respected. Socio-emotional learning is given equal importance to academics; in the real world those skills are as important, if not more important, than academics for navigating the increasing complexities of the twenty-first century.

Bound up with a focus on specific outcomes and a centralized curriculum are the assessment systems that go along with them. As this book outlines, when assessment becomes more removed from the teacher's input, it often becomes more about controlling teachers than actually helping children. Standardized tests, as well as externally produced report cards, checklists and other assessment tools, are blunt instruments for helping children learn, and the negative impacts increase with the level of the stakes that are riding on them.

Authentic assessment assesses a child's achievement relative to what that particular child could do using a variety of instruments (portfolios, teacher notes, parent teacher interviews, benchmarks). When developed by the teachers using it, it is focused around really knowing a child's strengths and weaknesses and helping each individual child move forward. Teachers who truly know their students know what kind of praise, encouragement or criticism will spur them on. And when children see that their teachers know and care about them, they will work hard for that praise. Halifax Independent School proves every day that marks at the elementary level are not necessary for motivating children. There is nothing that can replace insightful comments from a teacher that let a child know that their teacher understands what they are trying to accomplish, and is invested in helping them get there. This kind of assessment brings children and their teachers closer together, strengthening their bond.

In Chapter 8, I showed how engaged, trusted teachers who work in a respectful, collaborative environment and have autonomy will do everything they can for the students in their charge, as they do at Halifax Independent School. Unfortunately this doesn't happen in every school. Stressed teachers who feel underappreciated, overworked and ignored will have a harder time appreciating a child who has memorized the textbook and loudly declares her boredom with what is going on. Teachers who are in a competitive environment where their livelihood may depend on their students' results will not be likely to share resources or wisdom with other teachers. And when teachers have to take second jobs because their salaries don't cover their student debts, they will likely have less energy to spend learning with their students. Engaged teachers will have the energy and the will to collaborate and develop creative, whole-school, continuing activities such as Mini-Society.

I firmly believe that every child deserves — and could have — an education that puts them first, that will prepare them for the challenges of the twenty-first century and that will foster their love of learning. My years at Halifax Independent School have convinced me that it is possible to have progressive education for every child — that what works at Halifax Independent School is not magic and doesn't have to cost the earth.

That belief is why I have written this book. Research has taught us so much about education since the beginning of the progressive education movement in the 1970s. Halifax Independent School, unlike many schools, has had the freedom to experiment and to evolve organically in a way that makes educational sense. In these pages, I have tried to show what works at Halifax Independent and why it works. I have outlined the barriers that GERM has created to progressive education, in the hopes that Canadian schools will not repeat these mistakes.

I believe that the characteristics of Halifax Independent School that are fundamental to its success are:
1. All progressive approaches, theme studies included, capitalize on the child's innate curiosity and desire to learn. The curriculum is very local, is planned by the teachers and gives children choice over what they learn and how they do it. The integration of all the basic subject areas means that children are learning skills through interesting topics, and are learning them organically, not split up in separate boxes. Outcomes are broad, and not grade or content specific — teachers have more flexibility to incorporate creativity, communication, collaboration and critical thinking throughout. This allows children to develop on their own timetable and great care is taken to ensure that the teachers know what each child needs at each stage. Hands-on learning in all areas, especially math, means that children are learning in a natural way through what often seems like play. This ensures that the school motto, "Learning and loving it," is always at the forefront of any study.

2. Structured originally as a cooperative, teachers at Halifax Independent School have always had autonomy over all the major decisions affecting them, including curriculum, assessment, school policies, job conditions, hiring and more. Working in close conjunction with parents, this has made the school a real community, and the emphasis on respect for all has meant that teachers have felt respected for their expertise and trusted to do their work. Because of the ample collaboration and equality among the staff (with the head teacher a leader

among equals) an atmosphere of shared responsibility has developed, resulting in a challenging, vibrant work environment where everyone is committed to constantly making the school a better place. Halifax Independent teachers tend to love their jobs and stay a long time, and this has resulted in consistent staff who really know the students and their families. The lack of a central school board that controls staffing issues, mandates policies and supplies materials (among many other things) means that Halifax Independent has a lot more work to do, but the active parents and teachers working together on a variety of committees have more than compensated for this.

3. Halifax Independent's focus on the whole child, and acknowledgement that socio-emotional learning is just as important for a child's development as academic learning is a key part of its philosophy. Staff and parents spend considerable time establishing a climate that ensures the hidden curriculum of the school is closely allied with the explicit curriculum. This involves consciously creating a community (multi-age classes, cooperative structure, respect for all) where teachers really know their students, and give their emotional health a high priority.

4. Almost every chapter in this book mentions the importance of small classes: for good hands-on, inquiry teaching so that all students can benefit from the first-hand experiences; for authentic assessment so that teachers can keep track of their students' progress, especially in math and literacy, and give

them extra support or challenge when needed; to provide more opportunities for each child to shine whether it be in music, "starring" in a play, speaking out in French class or making a speech at Fair; for paying attention to each child's socio-emotional development and needs; for communicating with families and other teachers about each child; and, finally, so as not to overwhelm the teachers with all the requirements of doing all of the above and the record-keeping associated with it. At Halifax Independent, we have found that between fourteen and eighteen children in a class is ideal for elementary — too small can create some social problems.

5. Halifax Independent School has under two hundred students, and I have loved getting to know all the students and their families, and being part of a staff that works closely together in a supportive way. When I started there, the school had thirty-seven children and three teachers (that was really small!), but for years we hovered around the 80 to 120 mark, and we were a true family. As the school grew, we had to be vigilant about establishing new lines of communication and new policies to ensure that this was not lost — and I know that there will be a size at which this will become difficult, if not impossible. My only regret about Halifax Independent is that our students come from a wide geographical area — if its community encompassed a distinct neighbourhood and the community around it, it would be even better. I think that around two hundred children or less is an ideal number for an elementary school. Above that,

the number of teachers required may be too large for a truly collegial, supportive and democratic atmosphere.

6. The authentic assessment developed at Halifax Independent allows the teachers the freedom to teach the way they want to, yet at the same time helps them closely monitor each child to make sure they are moving forward and fully developing their abilities. I have shown that the lack of external tests or marks contributes to the intrinsic motivation that encourages children to take responsibility over their own learning and love doing it. The collaboration involved in developing the assessment measures (as well as the peer assessment the teachers do of themselves) contributes to a sense of ownership, and ensures that it can change to meet changing needs.

Do I think that all schools in Canada can or want to become just like Halifax Independent? That is not what this book is about. What I would like to see is that each child gets the best school for them, and that can happen when education puts the whole child at the centre. It happens at Halifax Independent School because it has autonomy, and because it is progressive — not just because it is an independent school. I believe that, in Canada, we have a public education system that is committed to equity and to constant improvement; we need to support that aspect, support the teachers who are on the frontlines and fan the flames of progressivity when we see them. When that happens we will see progressive education flourish, because that is what most teachers really want to do.

And there is reason to be optimistic about the future. In a small town in New Brunswick, I recently met two public school Grade 1 teachers and their principal who were teaching their children using the outdoors as their laboratory, spending the larger part of the school day outside. These teachers were lucky to have the autonomy to develop a local curriculum; they tailored it to their community, had the trust and respect of the parents and the principal, and with more sharing and collaboration, they may convince other teachers to join in. They are truly engaged professionals who will give their students a wonderful start to school.

These New Brunswick teachers and parents are harbingers of change. Having the support of the principal is important, but it's also vital to have a flexible administration that is not hogtied by rigid curriculum guidelines and centrally dictated outcomes. These teachers and parents are trying something they (and I) know is a better way for their children, and that can work right across this country.

When we let go of the idea that central control over education is desirable, we will see more and more of this kind of creativity in schools. I have also visited Equinox School in Toronto, just one of many "alternative" schools within the public system, where children learn in a holistic way that "recognizes that to become a full person, a growing child needs to develop — in addition to intellectual skills — physical, psychological, emotional, interpersonal, moral and spirited potentials."[119]

In Saskatoon, the school board has launched its first intergenerational classroom at a long-term care facility. Twenty-four Grade 6 students spend the year working on in-depth writing projects that will involve learning from the resident seniors or "elders," but they will also teach the elders about modern technology. There are many benefits for all; not least are the resources in the community care facility that are open to the children (the greenhouse, butterfly room, art studios), and the opportunity for the seniors to share their skills and wisdom.

Whenever I visit Halifax Independent School now, I am always amazed at how fast things change there. We used to have a running joke about how we would try something new, and if it succeeded, the next year it would be called a "tradition" and the parents and children would clamour for it to be repeated. This would go on for several years until eventually it would be replaced by a new "tradition." I think this is the mark of a truly dynamic school, where parents and teachers are engaged in innovating and learning together — a true community of learners.

But that kind of change comes from the bottom up. It is not the top-down change that in recent years bureaucrats have often imposed, and then, perhaps because of the huge expense incurred, set in stone.

Is Halifax Independent School really the "best school in the world"? Certainly some of the children and their parents have felt that over the years, and it has been a place where I, and my fellow teachers, have thrived. Former students have grown into successful, well-rounded adults, and the school's commitment to the "whole child" is becoming more widely known. But it is just one example of a progressive school, and when I envision every child in the best school for them, I picture a country with a host of progressive schools, all different, all springing from the community they belong to, but all sharing a commitment to learning and loving it.

ACKNOWLEDGEMENTS

This book has been bubbling away throughout my entire adult life and there are many people who have helped stir the pot . . . starting with my family — my brothers with whom I've had many lively talks about education, my parents, who didn't send me off to boarding school when they might have been pardoned for doing so and my two daughters, Kirsten Hurd and Winnie Bower, both of whom had a few educational experiments tried on them, but who turned out spectacularly well in spite of it.

My first years at the little Dal school, which became Halifax Independent School, were a revelation, overturning almost everything I thought I knew about education. Cate Allen and Heather Beall, my longtime colleagues, were a key part of this. But every HIS teacher, past and present, has been part of my education — in particular, Heather Johnson, Mandai Mohan, Maggie Duinker, Tania DesRoches, Jill Morgan, Leigh-Ann Fulmore, Laura Mikkelson, Cindy Cameron and Cleo Burke shared insights and feedback when I needed it most. Valerie Walker, wordsmith extraordinaire, often provided the "bon mot" and lots of technical support. And of course, the children and their parents were a constant source of joy throughout the years.

There have been many other educators who shared their wisdom with me, chiefly early pioneers at the school, Ruth Gamberg, Winnie Kwak and Meredith Hutchings who helped me understand the origins of theme studies. Others were generous with their time and expertise: Mary Carlson,

Judith Newman, Lois McVannell, Mark Cuming, Vanessa Fraser, Rita Bertoldi, Richard Messina, Linda Goldwater and Anne Everts.

I find writing a difficult, solitary process, but there were some fellow writers who enlivened the solitude and gave me hope: Joanne Light, Carol Anne Wien, Gwen Davies and other members of her writing class, my stepson Spencer Osberg, and at the crazy end, editor Jenn Harris.

But my husband Lars Osberg was the constant source of inspiration, the champion, the critic, the consoler, the refiner of vague ideas, the debunker of bad ones and the nurturer of good ones — this book owes its life in large part to him.

ENDNOTES

1. Ruth Gamberg, Winnifred Kwak, and Meredith Hutchings, *Learning and Loving It: Theme Studies in the Classroom* (Toronto: Ontario Institute for Studies in Education, 1988).
2. Dr. Jennifer Irwin (presentation, American University, Washington D.C.).
3. Pasi Sahlberg, *Finnish Lessons* (New York: Teachers College Press, 2010).
4. Programme of International Student Assessment (PISA), Organisation for Economic and Co-operative Development (OECD).
5. Organisation for Economic and Co-operative Development, *PISA 2015: Results in Focus* (Paris: OECD Publishing, 2016): 4.
6. Sir Ken Robinson, *Do Schools Kill Creativity?*, video, 19:24, 2006, https://www.ted.com/talks/ken_robinson_says_schools_kill_creativity?language=en.
7. Clean Nova Scotia, "Quagmire: A Simulation Game for Wetland Decision Making," (teacher resource, Dartmouth, NS, 2006), http://resources4rethinking.ca/media/Quagmire-Wetland-Game.pdf.
8. Gamberg et al., *Learning and Loving It*.
9. "'Play is the Work of the Child' Maria Montessori," *Childhood Development Institute*, accessed December 19, 2016, http://dev.mainelyseo.com/cdi/child-development/play-work-of-children/.
10. Richard R. Hake, "Interactive-Engagement versus Traditional Methods: A Six-Thousand-Student Survey of Mechanics Test Data for Introductory Physics Courses," *American Journal of Physics* 66, no. 1 (1998), doi: 10.1119/1.18809.
11. Jody L. Riskowski, Carrie Davis Todd, Bryan Wee, Melissa Dark, and Jon Harbor, "Exploring the Effectiveness of an Interdisciplinary Water Resources Engineering Module in an Eighth Grade Science Class," *International Journal of Engineering Education* 25 no. 1 (2009): 181–95, https://news.uns.purdue.edu/x/2009a/090128DarkStudy.html.

12. Riskowski et al., "Exploring the Effectiveness."
13. Gerald Lieberman and Linda Hoody, *Closing the Achievement Gap — Using the Environment as an Integrating Context for Learning*, State Education and Environment Round Table (Washington, D.C.: Council of Chief State School Officers, 1998), http://files.eric.ed.gov/fulltext/ED428943.pdf.
14. "Tenets for Learning in a School of Creativity: Inquiry-based Learning," *Calgary Board of Education*, accessed January 17, 2017, http://schools.cbe.ab.ca/b209/inquirybased.htm.
15. "The Project Approach," *Project Approach Teacher Educator Network*, accessed December 19, 2016, http://www.projectapproach.org.
16. Shelagh A. Gallagher, "Problem-Based Learning," (Unionville, NY: Royal Fireworks Publishing Company, 2015), http://www.rfwp.com/samples/engaged-educated-keynote.pdf.
17. "Teaching and Learning through Doreen Nelson's method of Design-Based Learning," *California State Polytechnic University*, last modified December 16, 2009, http://www.cpp.edu/~dnelson/.
18. *Education in Finland: Finnish education in a nutshell*, (Finnish Ministry of Education and Culture, 2013), http://www.minedu.fi/export/sites/default/OPM/Julkaisut/2013/liitteet/Finnish_education_in_a_nuttshell.pdf.
19. Alberta Learning, *Focus on inquiry: a teacher's guide to implementing inquiry-based learning* (Edmonton, AB: Learning Resources Centre, 2004), https://open.alberta.ca/publications/0778526666.
20. Paul J. Veugelers and Angela L. Fitzgerald, "Effectiveness of School Programs in Preventing Childhood Obesity: A Multilevel Comparison," *American Journal of Public Health* 95 no. 3 (2005): 432–35.
21. Benazir was a five-year-old who was fascinated with the printed word. Her teacher recognized this and gave her many opportunities to explore it. She therefore read at an early age, seamlessly, organically and enjoyably, thus giving her the impression that the teacher was "sneaking the learning in."
22. Pirjo Sinko, *Main factors behind the good PISA reading results in Finland*, Finnish National Board of Education (Helsinki: IFLA, 2012).

23. Compiled from PISA studies, Organisation for Economic and Co-operative Development.
24. BBC, *Beyond the Reading Wars*, podcast audio, Reading between the Lines, Adobe Flash, 28:00, June 3, 2012, http://www.bbc.co.uk/programmes/b01j74zc.
25. Sebastion P. Suggate, Elizabeth A. Schaughency, and Elaine Reese, "Children Learning to Read Later Catch Up to Children Reading Earlier," *Early Childhood Research Quarterly* 28 no. 1 (2012): 33–48.
26. Elizabeth Abbott, "Rock'n'reading", *Globe and Mail*, November 4, 2010, http://www.theglobeandmail.com/arts/books-and-media/rocknreading/article1216236/
27. Barbel Inhelder, Harold Chipman, and Charles Zwingmann, *Piaget and His School: A Reader in Developmental Psychology* (New York: Springer-Verlag, 1976): 11–23.
28. Judith M. Newman, *Whole Language: Theory in Use* (Portsmouth, NH: Heinemann Educational Books, 1985), Frank Smith, *Understanding Reading: A Psycholinguistic Analysis of Reading and Learning to Read* (Toronto: Holt, Rinehart and Winston, 1971).
29. Bill Martin, Jr., and Eric Carle, *Brown Bear, Brown Bear, What Do You See?* (New York: Doubleday, 1967).
30. Go Phonics, *The Fat Cat – Short Vowel Stories*, Level 2 Storybook (Foundations for Learning, 2000).
31. Sarah Smilansky and Leah Sheftaya, *Facilitating Play: A Medium for Promoting Cognitive, Socio-Emotional and Academic Development in Young Children* (Gaithersburg, MD: Psychosocial and Educational Publications, 1990).
32. Gamberg et al, *Learning and Loving It*.
33. Diane Stephens, *What matters? A Primer for Teaching Reading* (Portsmouth, NH: Heinemann Educational Books, Inc., 1990).
34. Dr. Seuss, *The Lorax* (New York: Random House, 1971).
35. House of Commons Education and Skills Committee, *Teaching Children to Read: Eighth Report of Session 2004–05* (London: House of Commons, 2005), 17.
36. National Institute of Health, *Report of the National Reading Panel: Teaching Children to Read* (US Department of Health and Human Services, 2000), https://www.nichd.nih.gov/publications/pubs/nrp/Pages/smallbook.aspx.

37. Joanne Yatvin, "Babes in the Woods: the Wanderings of the National Reading Panel," *Phi Delta Kappan* 83 no. 5 (2002), doi: 10.1177/003172170208300509.

38. Elaine Garan, *Resisting Reading Mandates: How to Triumph with the Truth* (Toronto: Pearson Education Canada, 2002); Gerald Coles, *Reading the Naked Truth: Literacy, Legislation and Lies* (Portsmouth, NH: Heinemann, 2003).

39. Ina Mullis, Michael Martin, Ann Kennedy, and Pierre Foy, *PIRLS 2006 International Report* (Boston: International Association for the Evaluation of Educational Achievement, 2007): 141, http://timss.bc.edu/pirls2006/intl_rpt.html.

40. Dale Johnson, Bonnie Johnson, Stephen Farenga, and Daniel Ness, *Stop High Stakes Testing: An Appeal to America's Conscience* (Lanham, MD: Rowman and Littlefield, 2007).

41. Padma Ravichandran, Brandel France de Bravo, and Rebecca Beaufort, "Young children and screen time," *National Centre for Health Research*, last modified 2016, http://center4research.org/child-teen-health/early-childhood-development/young-children-and-screen-time-television-dvds-computer/.

42. Sharon Friesen, "Math: Teaching it Better," *Education Canada* 46 no. 1 (2006): 6–10, http://www.cea-ace.ca/sites/cea-ace.ca/files/EdCan-2006-v46-n1-Friesen.pdf.

43. *Halifax Independent School*, last modified 2017, http://halifax-independentschool.ca.

44. Evelyn J. Sowell, "The Effects of Manipulatives in Mathematics Instruction," *Journal for Research in Mathematics Education* 20 no. 5 (1989): 498–505.

45. Joonkoo Park and Elizabeth Brannon, "Training the Approximate Number System Improves Math Proficiency," *Psychological Science* 24 no. 10 (2013): 2013–19.

46. Ariel Starr, Melissa Libertus, and Elizabeth Brannon, "Number Sense in Infancy Predicts Mathematical Abilities in Childhood," *Proceedings of the National Academy of Sciences* 110 no. 45 (2013): 18116–20.

47. Caroline Alphonso, "Canada's Fall in Math-Education Ranking Sets Off Alarm Bells," *Globe and Mail*, December 3, 2013.

48. Organisation for Economic and Co-operative Development, *PISA 2012 Results: What Students Know and Can Do — Student*

Performance in Mathematics, Reading and Science, vol. 1, rev. ed. (Paris: OECD Publishing, 2014).

49. OECD, *PISA 2015:* 14.
50. Anna Stokke, "What to Do about Canada's Declining Math Scores?" *CD Howe Institute Commentary* no. 427 (2015).
51. Moira MacDonald, "Decline of Canadian Students' Math Skills the Fault of 'Discovery Learning': C.D. Howe Institute," *National Post*, May 27, 2015.
52. Alberta Government, *Bulletin for Teachers: Helping Parents Understand the Alberta Mathematics Kindergarten to Grade 9 Program of Studies* (2015), https://education.alberta.ca/media/481796/teacher_bulletin.pdf.
53. Friesen, "Math."
54. "KU research establishes link between music education and academic achievement," *University of Kansas News*, January 15, 2014, https://news.ku.edu/2014/01/14/ku-research-establishes-link-between-music-education-and-academic-achievement.
55. Kathryn Vaughan and Ellen Winner, "SAT Scores of Students Who Take Arts: What We Can and Cannot Conclude about the Association," *Journal of Aesthetic Education* 34 no. 3/4 (2000): 77–89.
56. J. Hudziak et al., "Cortical Thickness Maturation and Duration of Music Training: Health-Promoting Activities Shape Brain Development," *Journal of the American Academy of Child and Adolescent Psychiatry* 53 no. 11 (2014): 1153–61.
57. Lois McVannell, interview by author.
58. Rena Upitis, *Arts Education and the Development of the Whole Child* (Kingston: Queen's University Press, 2011).
59. In only ten years, from 1999 to 2009, the number of elementary schools with specialist music teachers in Ontario shrank by a third. Over one third of elementary schools in Ontario fundraise to support arts programs and over 80 per cent of these are in larger schools in cities, mostly in wealthier neighbourhoods.
60. In Toronto in the 2012–13 school year, the top twenty public schools fundraised about $3.9 million and the bottom twenty raised $44,000. The Jackman Public School in Riverdale, one of the richest communities in Toronto, fundraised $100,000 one year and spent the money on SMART Boards, iPads

and arts enrichment for the children. In addition to having a wealthy parent body to draw on for fundraising, this school also has well connected and talented parents whose skills are called on — one parent's local rock group performs regularly for school benefits.

61. Kelly Gallagher-Mackay et al., *Annual Report on Ontario's Publicly Funded Schools 2013* (Toronto: People for Education, 2013), http://www.peopleforeducation.ca/wp-content/uploads/2013/05/annual-report-2013-WEB.pdf.

62. Allan Anderson and Dennis Tupman, "Music education in British Columbia," in *From Sea to Sea: Perspectives on Music Education in Canada*, eds., Kari Veblen et al. (London, ON: Western Libraries, University of Western Ontario, 2007), http://ir.lib.uwo.ca/musiceducationebooks/1.

63. Max Cooke, "A Collision of Culture, Values and Education Policy: Scrapping Early French Immersion in New Brunswick," *Education Canada* 49 no. 2 (2010), http://www.cea-ace.ca/sites/cea-ace.ca/files/EdCan-2009-v49-n2-Cooke.pdf.

64. *Linguistic Characteristics of Canadians*, Statistics Canada, last modified December 12, 2015, https://www12.statcan.gc.ca/census-recensement/2011/as-sa/98-314-x/98-314-x2011001-eng.cfm.

65. Jan Vanhove, "The Critical Period Hypothesis in Second Language Acquisition: A Statistical Critique and a Reanalysis," *PLoS One* 8, no. 7 (2013), doi: 10.1371/journal.pone.0069172.

66. Sharon Lapkin, "Imagining Core French in the 21st Century," (June paper presented at the Colloquium on Bilingualism in a Plurilingual Canada: Research and Implications Official Languages and Bilingualism Institute, University of Ottawa, 2008).

67. Aaron Hutchins, "Just Say 'Non': The Problem with French Immersion," *MacLean's*, March 22, 2015.

68. Canadian Parents for French, *The State of French Second Language Education 2012: Fact Sheet for Parents*, http://cpf.ca/en/files/Parent.pdf.

69. OECD, *PISA 2015*: 10.

70. Douglas Willms, "The Case for Universal French Instruction," *Canadian Research Institute for Social Policy Policy Brief*, April 2008.

71. Fred Genesee, "What do we Know about Bilingual Education for Majority Students," in *Handbook of Bilingual Education*, ed. Tej Bhatia (Malden, MA: Blackwell, 2004).

72. Mari Wesche, "Early French Immersion — How has the Original Canadian Model Stood the Test of Time?" in *An Integrated View of Language Development: Papers in Honor of Henning Wode*, eds. Petra Burmeister, Thorsten Piske, and Andreas Rohde (Trier, Germany: Wissenschaftlicher Verlag Trier, 2002).

73. James Croll and Patricia Lee, *Report of the French Second Language Commission* (Fredericton, NB: Department of Education, 2008).

74. Willms, "Universal French Instruction."

75. Joseph Dicks, *The Case for Early French Immersion — A Response to J. Douglas Willms*, rev. ed. (Fredericton, NB: Second Language Research Institute of Canada [L2RIC], University of New Brunswick, May 5, 2008), http://www.unb.ca/fredericton/second-language/_resources/pdf/lricnotes/spring2008.pdf.

76. Molly Hurd, "Minority Language Children and French Immersion: Additive Multilingualism or Subtractive Semi-lingualism?" *Canadian Modern Language Review* 49, no. 3 (April 1993): 514–25.

77. Jessica Ball, *Enhancing Learning of Children from Diverse Language Backgrounds: Mother Tongue-Based Bilingual or Multilingual Education in Early Childhood and Early Primary School Years* (Paris: UNESCO, 2011), http://unesdoc.unesco.org/images/0021/002122/212270e.pdf.

78. Sarah C. Gudchinsky, *Literacy in the Mother Tongue and Second Language Learning* (Laval, QC: International Center for Research on Bilingualism, Laval University, 1971), http://files.eric.ed.gov/fulltext/ED060753.pdf.

79. Lapkin, "Imagining Core French."

80. Lapkin, "Imagining Core French."

81. Alina MacFarlane, *An Examination of Intensive French: A Pedagogical Strategy for the Improvement of French as a Second Language Outcomes in Canada* (Canadian Association of Second Language Teachers, 2005), http://www.caslt.org/pdf/IF.pdf.

82. *Halifax Independent School*, http://halifaxindependentschool.ca.
83. Ranjit Singh Malhi, "Self-Esteem and Academic Achievement," *Total Quality Management* (2010), http://www.tqm.com.my/web/05_bookArticle_11.html.
84. Amy Chua and Jed Rubenfeld, *The Triple Package: How Three Unlikely Traits Explain the Rise and Fall of Cultural Groups in America* (New York: Penguin Books, 2014).
85. Robert Fulghum, *All I Really Need to Know I Learned in Kindergarten* (New York: Villard Books, 1990).
86. "Restorative Approaches," *National Centre for Restorative Approaches*, accessed January 12, 2017, http://www.transformingconflict.org/content/restorative-approaches-0.
87. Common Core, State Standards Initiative, *Learn about the Common Core in Three Minutes*, video, 03:00, accessed January 12, 2017, http://www.corestandards.org/video/.
88. Percy Buffington, "Competition vs. Cooperation," *Charles Warner*, accessed January 12, 2017, http://www.charleswarner.us/articles/competit.htm.
89. Organisation for Economic Co-operation and Development, "Social Capital," *Glossary of Statistical Terms*, last modified March 13, 2014, https://stats.oecd.org/glossary/detail.asp?ID=3560.
90. Priscilla Pardini, "The Slowdown of Multi-age Classrooms," *American Association of School Administrators*, accessed January 12, 2017, https://www.aasa.org/SchoolAdministratorArticle.aspx?id=8720.
91. Macarena Ares Abalde, "School Size Policies: A Literature Review," *OECD Education Working Papers*, no. 106 (Paris: OECD Publishing, November 2014), doi: 10.1787/5jxt472ddkjl-en.
92. Barbara Kent Lawrence, quoted in "Ontario School Closures: What's Standing in the Way of the 'Dollars & Sense' Alternative?" *Educhatter's Blog*, February 22, 2015, https://educhatter.wordpress.com/2015/02/22/ontario-school-closures-whats-standing-in-the-way-of-the-dollars-sense-alternative/.
93. Ann Egalite and Brian Kisida, "The Impact of School Size on Student Achievement: Evidence from Four States, EDR Working Paper. May 2013, https://www.

lwsd.org/SiteCollectionDocuments/News/Long-Term-Facilities-Planning-Task-Force/2015.04.15/Summary-of-School-Size-Research.pdf

94. National Centre for Education Statistics, "Education Indicators: An International Perspective," https://nces.ed.gov/pubs/eiip/eiipid23.asp

95. "Safe and Accepting Schools: Promoting a Positive School Climate," *Ontario Ministry of Education*, last modified March 25, 2014, http://www.edu.gov.on.ca/eng/parents/climate.html.

96. "On average teachers are spending a day per week, in total, on some form of assessment . . . The increased time spent on various forms of assessment might therefore be a major factor in explaining the increase in overall workload from around 44 hours a week, prior to the introduction of the National Curriculum, and the present estimate of around 55 hours." Maurice Galton et al., *A Life in Teaching? The Impact of Change on Primary Teachers' Working Lives* (National Union of Teachers, 2002).

97. OECD, "Education Indicators in Focus," (2012) pg. 2, https://www.oecd.org/education/skills-beyond-school/Education%20Indicators%20in%20Focus%207.pdf.

98. "Authentic Assessment Overview," *Teacher Vision*, accessed January 12, 2017, https://www.teachervision.com/teaching-methods-and-management/educational-testing/4911.html.

99. Education Quality and Accountability Office, *The Power of Ontario's Provincial Testing Program*, (Toronto: Education Quality and Accountability Office, 2012) http://www.eqao.com/en/assessments/communication-docs/power-provincial-testing-program.pdf.

100. Frances Willick, "Parents Weary of Report Card 'Mumbo-Jumbo'," *Chronicle Herald*, July 2, 2013, www.thechronicleherald.ca/novascotia/1139441-parents-weary-of-report-card-mumbo-jumbo.

101. Tracy Hounsell, interview, CTV, May 30, 2014.

102. Teresa Amabile and Steve Kramer, "What Doesn't Motivate Creativity Can Kill It," *Harvard Business Review*, April 25, 2012.

103. Pasi Sahlberg, *Finnish Lessons* (New York: Teachers College Press, 2010): 46.

104. Raj Chetty et al, "Measuring the Impact of Teachers II: Value-added and Student Outcomes in Adulthood," (National Bureau of Economic Research, September 2013) http://www.irs.princeton.edu/sites/irs/files/event/uploads/Impact%20of%20Teachers%20Part%202.pdf.

105. Education at a Glance, OECD, 2014

106. "Supporting Teacher Professionalism: Insights from TALIS 2013," OECD, accessed January 13, 2017, http://www.keepeek.com/Digital-Asset-Management/oecd/education/supporting-teacher-professionalism_9789264248601-en#page25.

107. Sahlberg, *Finnish Lessons*: 7.

108. Steven Covey, *The 7 Habits of Highly Effective People*, 1989, Franklin Covey.

109. Education at a Glance, OECD, 2016, page 271.

110. "Teachers in Finland — trusted professionals," (Finnish National Board of Education) accessed January 27, 2017, http://www.oph.fi/download/148962_Teachers_in_Finland.pdf.

111. Sahlberg, *Finnish Lessons*: 90

112. Harry Smaller et al., "Canadian Teachers' Learning Practices and Workload Issues: Results from a National Teacher Survey and Follow-Up Focus Groups," (paper, Research Network on Work and Lifelong Learning Conference, June 2005).

113. Morgan Polikoff and Andrew Porter, "State Value-Added Performance Measures Do Not Reflect the Content or Quality of Teachers' Instruction," *Educational Evaluation and Policy Analysis*, March 13, 2014, http://www.aera.net/Newsroom/NewsReleasesandStatements/StudyStateValue-AddedPerformanceMeasuresDoNotReflecttheContentor-QualityofTeachers%E2%80%99Instruction/tabid/15512/Default.aspx.

114. Yvan Guillemette, "School Class Size: Smaller isn't Better," *CD Howe Institute Commentary* no. 215 (August 2005), https://www.cdhowe.org/public-policy-research/school-class-size-smaller-isnt-better.

115. Eric Hanushek, "The Evidence on Class Size," in *Earning and learning: How schools matter*, edited by Susan E. Mayer and

Paul E. Peterson (Washington, DC: Brookings Institution): 131–168

116. Peter Blatchford et al., "The Effect of Class Size on the Teaching of Pupils Aged 7–11 Years," *School Effectiveness and Improvement* 18 no. 2 (May 2007): 147–172.

117. Canadian Council on Learning, "Lessons in Learning: Making Sense of the Class Size Debate," September 2005, accessed January 17, 2017.

118. John Hattie, "195 Influences and Effect Sizes Related to Student Achievement," *Visible Learning*, http://visible-learning.org/hattie-ranking-influences-effect-sizes-learning-achievement/.

119. Ron Miller, quoted in "About Our School," *Equinox Holistic Alternative School*, https://equinoxschool.ca/about/.

INDEX

A

academic achievement
    and class size, 228
    and instructional time, 225-226
    and school size, 186-187
    and standardized assessment, 195
    early childhood education correlation, 89
    experiential learning correlation, 40
    measurement of, 59
    music education correlation, 121
    self-esteem correlation, 161

age segregation in schools, 23-24, 181-184. *See* multi-age classrooms

Alberta, 49-51, 54, 111

alternative assessment. *See* authentic assessment

approximate number system, 101-102

arts education, 41, 120-137, 232-238, 240-241, 247

authentic assessment, 163, 190-191, 196-202, 209-213, 218

B

balanced literacy education, 65-67, 76, 83, 85, 92

benchmarks, 197-198, 200

behaviourist approach. *See* traditional education

bilingualism, 138-140, 145, 152-153

British Columbia, 149-150

British National Literacy Strategy, 84

budgets. *See* resource allocation

Buffington, Percy, 179

bullying prevention, 165

business skills, 232-250

C

Canada
    arts education, 135-136
    assessment methods, 205-206
    equity in education, 16-17
    French as a second language programs, 139-140
    literacy education, 83
    mathematics instruction, 96
    PISA scores, 16, 109-110
    provincial curricula, 54-55
    school size, 184
    standardized tests, 15-16
    teacher salaries, 221

Canadian Teachers Federation, 221

CD Howe Institute, 228

Chard, Sylvia, 51

Clandfield, David 188

class composition, 227

class size, 37, 85, 115-116, 227-229

classroom design, 167-168
community hub schools, 188
competition, 34, 160, 179, 206, 226, 256
computers in the classroom, 92, 100, 104, 114
conflict resolution, 156-166, 169-174, 181, 241-244, 249
consolidation of schools, 184-186
constructivism. *See* progressive education
cooperation, 18, 37, 81, 108, 128-134, 158, 160, 179-181, 184
creativity, 100, 120, 130-134, 208, 210, 212
curriculum centralization, 52-55, 182, 184-185, 193-196, 204, 217-220, 222, 251-255

D

democracy, 174-179
design-based learning, 52
differentiated instruction, 35, 100-102, 104, 182
Dweck, Carol, 162
dyslexia, 86-89

E

early childhood education, 57, 89
emotional intelligence, 158, 164-166, 170
education funding, 135-37, 203
Education Quality and Accountability office (EQAO), 205-206
Equinox Holistic Alternative School, 54

equity in education, 15-17, 110, 135, 143-144, 152, 193, 207, 229
Eric Jackman School, 14
experiential learning
    and academic achievement, 38-40
    and arts education, 124-134
    and engagement, 42-46
    and literacy education, 71-74, 78-82
    and mathematics instruction, 93-96, 102, 106-117
    and "Mini Society," 232-250
    and second language education, 148-149
    types of, 51-52

F

fees. *See* tuition and fees
field trips, 43-45
financial literacy, 232-250
Finland, 16-17, 53, 57-58, 110, 187, 204, 212, 218-219, 221, 223, 225, 226
French as a second language programs
    core French programs, 139, 148-151
    early French immersion programs, 139, 142-147, 152-154
    in Europe, 140
    late French immersion programs, 145-147, 151-154
    middle French immersion programs, 145-147

G

Gallagher, Sheila, 51
Global Education Reform Movement (GERM), 15-17, 59, 85, 202-203, 207, 220, 222
Great Britain, 14-16, 54, 57-58, 84-85, 87-88, 110, 160, 167, 174, 190, 194-196, 203-204, 219-220, 226

H

hands-on learning. *See* experiential learning
hidden curriculum, 159-160, 163-164, 166, 169, 179, 188-189
hierarchy in schools, 166-169, 180-181, 203
holistic education, 30, 41-42, 65, 158, 251-252

I

individual differences. *See* differentiated instruction
inquiry-based learning, 48-51
instructional materials, 46-47, 63, 65, 183
integration of subjects, 41-43, 67, 71-74, 116-117, 124-134, 140-141, 147-148, 232-250
intuitive sense of number. *See* approximate number system

L

learning disabilities. *See* dyslexia
learning motivation, 30, 34-35, 64-65, 104-106, 113, 141, 163, 182, 210
learning styles, 100-102, 104, 115, 182, 208
literacy education, 56-92, 130-134, 194-195, 232-237, 247

M

manipulatives, 96-97, 102-103, 105-106, 112
Manley, John, 109
mathematics instruction, 93-119, 132, 232-247
multi-age classrooms, 23-24, 181-184, 187
music education, 121-126, 128, 136
musical theatre, 128-134

N

National Reading Panel (NRP), 84
Nelson, Doreen, 52
New Brunswick, 145-146, 152
No Child Left Behind Act, 15, 84
Nova Scotia, 54-55, 165, 187-188, 209
Nova Scotia Small Schools Initiative, 187-188

O

Ontario, 54, 205-206
Ontario Institute for Studies in Education, 14

P

Pan-Canadian Assessment Program, 205
parent advisory groups, 55

parent participation in schools, 55, 136-137, 223-225
parent role, 38, 90-92, 118-119
parent-teacher interviews, 191, 197-199, 200, 209
participative decision-making, 36, 174-179, 236-237, 241-243
peer mediator programs, 170, 172
phonics-based literacy education, 61, 65-67, 70, 75, 83-84, 87
Piaget, Jean, 60
play, 34-35, 70-71, 103, 105-106
portfolio assessment, 197
problem-based learning, 51-52
problem-solving, 18, 40, 51-52, 94-96, 100-108, 112, 115, 157, 170-174, 177-178, 241-244, 249
Programme for International Student Assessment (PISA), 16-17, 51, 53, 56, 89, 162, 204, 212, 216
project-based learning, 40, 51, 140-141, 147-151. *See also* experiential learning

R

reading, 56-78, 84-92
reading readiness, 57, 59, 85
report cards, 162-63, 190-191, 197, 200, 205, 208-210, 212
research, 45-46, 48, 77
resource allocation, 11, 46, 186, 206
respect, 164-169, 171, 178, 220-221

retention of information, 38-39, 41
Robinson, Ken, 18
rural schools, 136-137, 143-144, 184-188

S

Sahlberg, Pasi, 212, 218-219, 221
school closures, 184-187
school size, 184-187
second language education, 138-154
self-assessment, 191, 200, 211
self-esteem, 161-164, 166, 184, 206
social capital, 180-181, 185
social skills, 158-160, 164-166, 169, 179-181
socio-emotional learning, 155-189
Speak Up program, 165
split classrooms, 182, 187
standardized assessment, 15, 53, 90, 190-196, 202-209, 212, 221
Stokke, Anna, 111

T

teacher administrator relationship, 166-167, 219
teacher autonomy, 53-55, 209, 216-223, 232
teacher burnout, 225
teacher collaboration, 198, 200-201, 209, 216, 223-227
teacher evaluation, 219-220, 226-227

teacher recruitment and retention, 219-220, 223
teacher role, 37, 115-116, 167-168, 214-216, 227-229, 230-231
teacher salaries, 203, 217, 221
tests, 15, 53, 90, 162-163, 192-196, 199, 200, 202-208
theme studies, 9, 24-28, 30-55, 64, 67, 71-75, 77-79, 116-117, 124-27, 141, 144, 153, 182, 197, 210
traditional assessment. *See* standardized assessment
time factors, 43, 73, 115-116, 160, 190, 206, 209, 216, 225-226
traditional education, 12-14, 29, 83, 95, 99, 104-105, 112-114, 116, 144
tuition and fees, 11, 135-136

U

United States of America, 15-16, 35, 54, 57-58, 84-85, 95, 110, 179, 184, 204, 226
US National Council of Teachers of Mathematics, 95

V

Value Added Model, 226
values education, 158-160, 164-169

W

whole child education. *See* holistic education
whole-language approach, 61-65, 71, 73, 83
WISE Math (Western Initiative for Strengthening Education in Math), 111
workplace skills, 232-247
writing, 76-82, 130-134

Y

Yatvin, Joanne, 84